The Making of the Iranian Community in America

Maboud Ansari

PARDIS PRESS, INC.
NEW YORK, N.Y.

Library of Congress Cataloging in Publication Data
Ansari, Maboud
Making of the Iranian Community in America
Bibliography: P
Includes Index
1. Iranians United States—Social Conditions Case Study
2. Maginality, Social—United States—Case Studies

1992 ISBN 0-9632600-0-6

To
Shaya and Pardis
with love and pride

Contents

LIST OF TABLES

About the Author

Maboud Ansari is a faculty member at the William Paterson College of New Jersey, where he has taught from 1971-73, 1975-78, and from 1984 to the present time. Born in Iran, he graduated with a B.A. (Persian Literature) at the Teachers' College of Tehran in 1964, and was subsequently awarded the degree of M.A. (Social Sciences) by the University of Tehran in 1968. He received his M.A. and Ph.D. degrees (Sociology) from the Graduate Faculty of the New School for Social Research in 1975.

Dr. Ansari returned to Iran in 1978 and joined the faculty of Reza Shah University. For the academic year, 1978-79, he was the chancellor of North University. From 1980-84, he was a research advisor for International Institute for Adult Literacy in Iran. During this period he personally conducted a survey on factors motivating adults to seek literacy in three provinces of Kerman, Sistan, and Isfahan.

In addition to various articles published in English and Farsi, Dr. Ansari has published *The Sociological Imagination* (trans. into Farsi, 1979) and co-authored (with Dr. H. Adibi) *Sociological Theory* (in Farsi, 1979). He has recently finished his translation of *Protestant Ethic and Spirit of Capitalism* and is being accepted for publication in Iran. His major academic and research interests include ethnic groups, social organizations, and cultural change, especially cultural changes in the Islamic Republic of Iran.

Dr. Ansari is currently writing two books: *Iranian Immigrants and Their Children: Ethnic Identity and Assimilation,* and *Revolution and Mass Mobilization: The Transformation of Political Culture in Iran.* This book is based on his eyewitness account of the revolution as well as on his field research during 1980-84 in Iran. His years of teaching and research, particularly counseling young Iranians in America, convinced Dr. Ansari to come up with the idea of publishing the first Iranian-American magazine. This magazine, PARDIS, is for and about Iranians in the United States.

Preface To The New Edition

This book contains the first attempt to give a comprehensive sociological account of the development of the Iranian community in the United States. The first edition of the book was originally published in 1988.

In the light of a continuing demand for the book, I decided to reprint it in this unconventional format without any revision. In a sense, a book of this character cannot be revised, since it deals with a social process in a given historical period. *The MAKING of the IRANIAN COMMUNITY in AMERICA* was conceived and designed as a companion to my first book, but due to circumstances, is now included as Part Three in this volume. It is hoped, these two distinctive field works, together, will assist the reader to better understand the historical development of the Iranian community in America.

Maboud Ansari, Ph.D.
West Orange, N.J.
September 1991

Preface To The First Edition

The primary object of this book is to explain those elements which seem to characterize Iranian immigrants residing in the United States. To be more specific, I seek to explain the situation of "dual marginality" among immigrant Iranian professionals.

The concept of dual marginality is developed from my own effort to explain the situation in which immigrants find themselves. It is my suggestion that those Iranians who came to this country initially as sojourners—with a strong feeling of belonging at home, and a firm conviction of returning—are subject to the experience of dual marginality. That is, they find themselves estranged from the host and the home society.

In this study, the dually marginal Iranian is defined as a would-be returnee to Iran who continues to remain an "uncertain," "undecided" *belataklif* sojourner in the United States. In this context, the dually marginal person is a product of economic, political, and cultural imperialism. He or she arises from colonial contact, Western penetration, and involuntary migration. In some Third World countries such historical events have produced alienated intellectuals and professionals, who upon their migration to Western countries became dually marginal persons. This is the situation of a number of immigrant Iranian professionals in the United States.

The field work on which this book is based was originally carried out during 1972-74. Supplemental research and the actual writing of the main part of this manuscript were undertaken in 1978. It is thus a book fixed in time and reflective of a period in which the field research was carried out.

Since the revolutionary movement of 1978 and the establishment of Iran's Islamic Republic, the Iranian community in the United States has undergone both qualitative and quantitative changes. These recent developments, as I shall outline in the epilogue to this study, have already affected certain aspects of the immigrants' life. Nevertheless I believe, after revisiting some of my former respondents and reviewing several newly published newspapers aimed at the Iranian community, that the analysis of dual marginality remains essentionally sound. The different currents of change do not seem to alter the central theme and significance of the findings of this volume. Indeed, the present situation of the vast majority of the immigrants illustrates, now more than ever, the empirical reality of dual marginality. In other words, the status of dual marginality of the uncertain immigrants has been reinforced because the revolutionary movement of 1978-79 did not create the "utopia" in which they could see the realization of their value system and of economic prosperity. At this point, I do not wish to extend my interpretation beyond the specific data of the original study. However, in the epilogue to which I have referred, I shall briefly explore the obvious changes since the drafting of the present manuscript in the summer of 1978. These changes will be examined in more detail in a subsequent volume which will reflect my follow-up study of this community, and place its emphasis on the second-generation of Iranian-Americans.

It should be noted that the present study was done in a period when the activities of SAVAK, the Shah's secret police, were extended beyond Iran's borders, and any expression of discontent with the Pahlavi regime could have caused serious trouble for the author on his return to Iran in the summer of 1978. For this reason, some of the annotation or statements may have suffered from the political climate during the period when the material was collected. This book should be understood in the light of these factors.

The intention of the study was both theoretical as well as empirical. In Part One the first two chapters provide a theoretical framework for the study and give an account of the broader historical process of Westernization of Iran. Chapter 3 presents as background to Iranian emigration, the pattern and the causes of that population movement.

Part Two is concerned primarily with quantitative and qualitative analysis of data. Chapter 4 describes the general characteristics of the members of the sample and their generally displayed orientations. In Chapter 5 the focus shifts from the individual immigrant to the community and its peculiar features. The last four chapters explain the immigrants' out-group relationships, their orientations toward the home society, and the Iranian parents' responses to the situation of their children. Finally, I draw some general conclusions about the condition of the Iranian community and the predominant orientation of immigrants by type toward their marginal positions in both societies.

PART I

Theoretical and Historical Developments

CHAPTER 1

The Problem of Dual Marginality

Marginality

The concept of marginality, rooted in sociological tradition, has not yet enjoyed a full exposition of its dimension. Despite fifty years of widespread discussion and effort to refine the concept, the fact is that its full potential as well as its empirical treatment with regard to new immigrants has not been fully examined.

Marginality so far rests upon the assumption that immigrants to a strange land will experience a sense of dislocation or exclusion, an inevitable by-product of their emigration. The immigrant hence is depicted as the paradigm case of the marginal person. That is, it is generally assumed that the immigrant, prior to his emigration, was a well-integrated or non-marginal member of his society with a definite and well-defined social position. Consequently, he became marginal only when he found himself in another society. While some sociologists have acknowledged the phenomenon of native marginality—that is, when natives under certain circumstances become marginals to their own society—there has been no empirical treatment of its implication in the case of native marginals who become immigrants in another society.

In this study it is my suggestion that at least some immigrants' marginality is often accompanied or extended by a prior condition at home. That is, the immigrant may arrive in another country as an already marginal member in his own society and then, under some circumstances, he may find himself in a different form of marginal situation in the host society. The concrete case of such a situation is that of the Iranian professional immigrants in the United States who are subject to the experience of dual marginality. This is the situation in which they find themselves marginal with respect to both societies.

Thus, to explain this phenomenon, a heretofore unnoticed type of marginality, we begin our analysis with a brief review of the "marginal man" concept as suggested by Robert E. Park in "Human

Migration and Marginal Man" and articulated by Everett Stonequist in *The Marginal Man*.

According to Park's formulation, the marginal man is a cultural hybrid who lives and shares intimately in the cultural life of two distinct peoples, unwilling to break with his past and yet not fully accepted by the inhabitants of the host society. Park writes:

> The marginal man is a personality type that arises at a time and a place where, out of the conflict of races and cultures, new societies, new peoples and cultures are coming into existence. The fate which condemns him to live, at the same time, in two worlds is the same which compels him to assume, in relation to the worlds in which he lives, the role of a cosmopolitan and a stranger. Inevitably he becomes, relatively to his cultural milieu, the individual with the wider horizon, the keener intelligence, the more detached and rational viewpoint.[1]

With regard to the situation in which the marginal man arises, Park notes that contemporary events favor the conflict of cultures, so that many situations arise where a person may be on the margins of two cultures. Regarding human migration as one of these decisive events, he states: "One of the consequences of migration is to create a situation in which the same individual—who may or may not be a mixed blood—finds himself striving to live in two diverse cultural groups. The effect is to produce an unstable character—a personality type with characteristic forms of behavior. This is the "marginal man."[2]

In relation to the effects on the mentality of the marginal man, Park maintains that, since the marginal man is influenced by a divided self, he experiences a sense of permanent crisis. Such crisis, especially for the immigrant, according to Park, involves a period of inner turmoil and intense self-consciousness. "The result is that he tends to become a personality type."[3]

Thus, with Park's original formulation, the phrase "marginal man' and the phenomenon it designates came formally into sociological literature, particularly the study of intercultural as well as interracial contacts In fact, it was through his wider interest in culture contacts and particularly the evolution of race relations that Park saw the case of the marginal man as a specific situation which might temporarily retard the progress of assimilation. In his sociology of the marginal man as in the rest of his sociology, Park tended to focus analytical attention on situations of specific events that upset the progress of what he called "the race-relation cycle."[4] He acknowledged that the marginal man was an effect of economic, political, and cultural imperialism, but he paid little attention to those circumstances that might have made the immigrant marginal both at home and in the host society. In short, Park's notion of the immigrant's marginality emerged directly from his interest in the immigrant's role as a generator of social contacts and in some of the social an psychological consequences of his situation in the host society.[5]

Although Robert E. Park was the first to use the terms "marginality" and "marginal man," the fullest exposition of the marginal man concept came from Park's student Everett Stonequist. Stonequist speaks of the marginal man as:

> ...one who is poised in psychological uncertainty between two (or more) social worlds; reflecting in his soul the discord and harmonies, repulsions and attractions of these worlds, or of which is often "dominant" over the other; within which membership is implicitly based upon birth or ancestry (race or nationality); and where exclusion removes the individual from a system of group relations.[6]

Accepting Park's broad statement on the marginal man, Stonequist goes further and indicates that while marginality is clearly seen in the case of the racial and cultural hybrid, it is also apparent in the relation minor groups, such as social classes, religious sects, and communities. In this respect he states: "The individual who through migration, education, marriage, or some other influence leaves one social group or culture without making a satisfactory adjustment to another finds himself on the margin of each but a member of neither. He is a "marginal man."[7]

Thus he distinguishes the different types of marginal man. In dealing with the cultural hybrid, who has emerged as a result of "the Europeanization of the globe," Stonequist includes cases of Europeanized Africans, Westernized Orientals, and denationalized Europeans. With regard to Westernized Indians, he maintains:

> Of all the culture contacts that India has had, that with the West has been the most profound. Other migrants into India have fused their interests with the country, but the British have maintained a baffling aloofness while continuing to govern and penetrate the country...Yet Westernization of the English variety has entered deeply into the Indian mind, and deeply disturbed the traditional rhythm of India's life.[8]

He goes on to say that the Western economic system, the British government, and the Christian church have been obvious forces of such cultural diffusion. "But even more disturbing, for the educated classes at least, has been the introduction of English education. It is through the English language and English literary education that we may look for the immediate source of much of India's spiritual disruption."[9]

Stonequist also emphasizes the psychological impact of the marginal situation on individual personality. The individual who arises in a marginal situation, according to him, is likely to display a dual personality, including personality traits such as a double consciousness, excessive consciousness, an inferiority complex, etc. But, pointing out the positive consequences of social marginality, he maintains:

> In general, the individual may evolve in several different directions. He may continue toward the dominant group and perhaps eventually succeed in becoming an accepted member. In this case the conflict ends, or merely echoes recurrently as a memory. This solution is more likely to occur where there is no biological barrier. "Passing" is a more uncertain solution. Another possibility lies in moving in the other direction, throwing one's lot with the subordinate group, if it in turn is willing. The marginal individual's dual contact may give him an advantage, making him a leader. Resentment may spur him to fight the dominant group; he becomes a "revolutionary," or aggressive nationalist.[10]

In short, although Stonequist goes beyond Park's formulation and becomes aware of a different kind of marginality resulting from Western penetration, he does not carry out a full-scale study of the marginal man whom he identifies in non-Western societies. He is primarily interested in delineating different kinds of marginal men and their personality characteristics. Therefore his exposition of the marginal man concept remains at the conceptual level, and does not inspire sociologists to examine the possibility of the dual marginality resulting from the migration of native marginal men. The situation of dual marginality, which is commonly exhibited by Iranian immigrants, can be stated as follows: "I am at home nowhere. In Iran I am a stranger *(biganeh)*; here in the United States I am an alien *(Khareji)*.

Critics of the Park-Stonequist Concept

The lack of clarity in the early formulation of the marginal man concept indicated a need for reformulation and reexamination of the concept. It was not, however, until 1941 that some major attempts were made in this direction.

The first qualification of the marginal man concept was made by Milton M. Goldberg. The concept around which his qualification was oriented was "marginal culture."[11] He argued that the inevitable product of a marginal situation is not necessarily a marginal man; one individual may have his own marginal culture and need not develop individual marginality.

Goldberg cites the American Jews as an example of a group with a marginal culture, a situation which, according to him, meets all the conditions. He maintains that the marginal culture of the second-generation Jew is a mixture of the cultural elements of immigrant Judaism provided by his family situation and of the elements contained in the wider gentile culture in which he must function.[12]

The sociological significance of the marginal culture of the second-generation Jew, according to Goldberg, is as follows:

> On the one hand, it allows him a normal form of participation in group activities, an opportunity for the expression of his own cultural interests...On the other hand, in so far as Jewish marginal culture produces a type individual definitely distinguishable from the members of dominant gentile culture by appearance (not necessarily physiological), mannerism, and inflection of speech, it is a contributing cause of anti-Semitism."[13]

With regard to the general application of the idea of marginal culture, Goldberg maintains that it is not necessarily applicable to all or even to a majority of the members of the culture. He explicitly points out that a marginal culture can develop within a significant proportion of a marginal group. Therefore, if we view marginal culture as a subculture, it seems to have some validity in the case of some of the Iranian immigrants in this country. For these Iranians marginal culture serves to provide meaning and continuity to their lives in a situation of personal marginality.[14]

In 1947 Arnold W. Green presented another reexamination of the marginal man concept.[15] He challenged Stonequist's argument that culture conflict, per se, is the basis of the personality characteristics of the marginal man. Green argues that group antagonism and not the disparity of culture items is the source of personality characteristics. It is Green's suggestion that the assumption that the marginal situation automatically generates response should be abandoned in favor of more rigorous investigation of the nature of that situation.[16]

It appears that Green's emphasis on group antagonism as one of the sources of personality characteristics is also relevant to the case of Iranian immigrants. As will be explained later, the marginality of Iranians in the United States stems from the disparity of culture items as well as from their group antagonism to the American political system.

Finally, in 1967, H. F. Dickie-Clark offered the first major empirical work on the marginal situation.[17] His work is essentially a report of sociological findings on social marginality among South African colored people. In this study Dickie-Clark defines the marginal situation as a hierarchical one of which the hallmark is some inconsistency in the ranking of matters regulated by the hierarchy. Thus, according to him, the marginal situation is a special case of hierarchical situations. What makes a hierarchical situation marginal in character is any inconsistency in the ranking of the individual or collectivity in any matter regulated by the hierarchical structure.[18]

With regard to the Durban coloreds, Dickie-Clark argues that the crucial fact of their marginality is not cultural differences but inconsistency between the cultural and social dimensions of the status hierarchy. According to him, the Durban coloreds are not culturally different from the dominant whites, because their cultural characteristics—their origin, culture, religion, language, and sometimes even their color—are the same as those of the whites.[19] It is in this regard that he claims that his definition of the marginal situation is "a strictly sociological one which deals with cultural and social statuses and ranking rather than biological characteristics, such as appearance, or psychological characteristics such as personality traits."[20]

One can of course question the major assumption of Dickie-Clark's study concerning a "complete" cultural parity of whites and coloreds in South Africa. But it must be acknowledged that this work with its emphasis on the cultural and social dimensions of the status hierarchy has greatly enlarged the scope of the marginal man formulation.

Moreover, it must be noted that Dickie-Clark's definition of the marginal situation seems to have some validity with respect to our present study. The Immigrant Iranian professionals as a group indeed constitute a status community characterized by inconsistency between the cultural and social dimensions of the status hierarchy of the two different societies. It is with respect to this point that Dickie-Clark's notion of the marginal situation seems to have some fruitful application for Iranians' marginal status group in this country.

Stranger and Homecomer

Our sociological awareness of the "stranger" as a marginal man traces back to the German sociologist Georg Simmel (1908) and is informed by the perceptive essay of Schutz.[21] The stranger, according to Simmel, is not just a wanderer "who comes today and goes tomorrow," having no specific structural position. On the contrary, he is a "person who comes today and stays tomorrow...He is fixed within a particular spatial group...but his position...is determined...by the fact that he does not belong to it from the beginning," and that he may leave again.[22] The stranger is one who is marginal to the group in which he participates, yet contributes to its existence by his presence. He imports qualities into the group which cannot stem from the group itself. According to Simmel it is the combination of nearness and distance that marks the relation of the stranger to the surrounding world.[23]

One consequence of the stranger's marginality, according to Simmel, is the "objectivity of the stranger." By virtue of his partial involvement in group affairs, the stranger is free to perceive things as they are and to observe surroundings with objectivity. Moreover, being distant and near at the same time, the stranger will often be called on as a confidant.

From a phenomenological perspective Alfred Schutz (1899-1959) also treats the stranger and the homecomer as marginal types. He writes:

> For our present purposes the term 'Stranger' shall mean an adult individual of our times and civilization who tries to be permanently accepted or at least tolerated by the group which he approaches.[24]

According to Schutz, the outstanding example of the stranger is an immigrant "who becomes essentially the man who has to place in question nearly everything that seems to be unquestionable to the members of the approached group."[25] From the point of view of the stranger, as Schutz notes, the host culture is "not a shelter but a field of adventure, not a matter of course but a questionable topic of investigation, not an instrument for disentangling problematic situations but a problematic situation itself and one hard to master."[26]

Moreover, the stranger, in Schutz's terminology, approaches the other group as a newcomer in the true meaning of the term. "At best he may be willing and able to share the present and future with the approached group in vivid and immediate experience; under all circumstances; however, he remains excluded from such experiences of its past. Seen from the point of view of the approached group, he is a man without a history.[27]

It seems that Simmel's and Schutz's conceptions of the stranger are also pertinent to the case of the American-returned middle class Iranian. When he returns to Iran, he finds himself a "familiar stranger" *(ashena-i biganeh)* Although he is in Iran, he does not find himself to be a participant member of his own society. That is, he is in society but not of it. As I shall explain later, his marginality involves awareness of exclusion from the exercise of his social, political, and professional rights.

The "homecomer" is another social type identified by Schutz. According to him, the returning veteran, the traveler, and the immigrant who returns to his native land, are all instances of homecomers.[28]

To the homecomer, as Schutz notes, life at home is no longer accessible in immediacy. "He has stepped, so to speak, into another social dimension not covered by the system of coordinates used as the scheme or reference for life at home. No longer does he experience as a participant in a vivid present the many we-relations which form the texture of the home group."[29]

Schutz's conception of the homecomer is indeed relevant to the case of the repatriated middle class Iranian. The majority of Iranian immigrants returning home at least once have suffered the typical shock described by Schutz. However, we tend to restrict Schutz's conception of the homecomer to those who return home to stay, not those who return for a temporary stay like some of the ambivalent Iranian immigrants in this study. By the Iranian homecomer I mean the individual who is able to function in various activities without suffering excessive or unbearable psychological stresses.[30]

The Sojourner

Another social type, and in many respects the most pertinent example to be mentioned here, is the sojourner, proposed by Paul C. P. Siu.[31] He treats the sojourner as a deviant type of the sociological form of the stranger. According to Siu, the essential characteristic of the sojourner is that he clings to the culture of his own ethnic group, in contrast to the bicultural complex of the marginal man. Psychologically he is unwilling to adjust as a permanent resident in the country of his sojourn. When he does, he becomes a marginal man."[32]

Siu states that both the marginal man and the sojourner are types of stranger—in Simmel's sense, products of the cultural frontier. His outstanding example of sojourner is the Chinese laundryman in the United States. However, he maintains that the sojourner concept may be applied to a whole range of foreign residents in any country to the extent that they maintain sojourner attitudes. "The colonist, the foreign trader, the diplomat, the foreign student, the international journalist, the foreign missionary, the research anthropologist abroad, and all sorts of migrant groups in different areas of the globe, in various degrees, may be considered sojourners in the sociological sense."[33]

The sojourner in Siu's sense views his sojourn as a "job" or a "mission "which is to be finished in the shortest possible time. Thus he usually organizes his life around accomplishing his goal. His job in the host society is tied up "with all sorts of personal needs for new experience, security, prestige, etc."[34]

With regard to his sojourn, the sojourner is likely to face a dilemma.

> Although the sojourner plans to get through with the job in the shortest possible time, yet he soon finds himself in a dilemma as to whether to stay abroad or return home. Naturally, this problem is related to the success or failure of the job—he would not like to return home without a sense of accomplishment and some sort of security. But this state is psychologically never achieved. In due time the sojourner becomes vague and uncertain about the termination of his sojourn because of the fact that he has already made some adjustments to his new environment and acquired an old-timer's attitude.[35]

In the larger society the sojourner remains as a spectator with no active participation. "Essentially his activities in the community (the host community) are symbiotic rather than social."[36] Contrary to the lack of out-group relations, the sojourner has a tendency to form in-group relationships. The sojourner and his countrymen very likely live together in a racial colony or cultural area. The colony is an instrument to establish some sort of primary-group relationships in the matrix of homeland culture. "Whatever activities the sojourner may participate in, in the community at large, in private life he tends to live apart from the natives and to share with his countrymen in striving to maintain homeland culture."[37]

With reference to his homeland, "the sojourner stays abroad, but he also never loses his homeland tie."[38] He stays several years, and, when opportunity permits, he takes a trip home for a visit. In his lifetime several trips are made back and forth, and in some cases the sojourn is terminated only by retirement or death. Siu concludes his essay by saying that "psychologically the sojourner is a potential wanderer, as Simmel puts it, who has not quite gotten over the freedom of coming and going."[39]

The final social types that need to be discussed are David Riesman's "open" and "secret" marginality types. In his essay "Some Observations Concerning-Marginality" Riesman proposes a dichotomy of marginality. He makes a distinction between what he calls "open marginality" and "secret marginality." Open marginality to him "is the kind that we read about in the writings of Park, that we are familiar with: the situation created when we have the educated Negro, the self-made man, the woman engineer, all the various kinds of marginality which have become, so to speak, institutionalized, defined."[40] The second type includes those who are marginal to their marginal groups. In other words, they do not feel as they are supposed to feel as inhabitants of that margin. They are the "passers" and those who defy the institutionalized definition of their own role.

Riesman's analytical discussion of dichotomy of marginality has also some validity with regard to the present study. It would seem that the situation of the Persian Yankee resembles that of "secret marginality." He usually does not share the feeling of marginality of other Iranians. That is, he remains marginal to the marginal group.

In relation to my study it must be noted that, while most of the discussions of marginality and its dimensions are generally pertinent to our case, they have a limited adequacy for the situation of the Iranian professional in the United States. It seems to me that such inadequacy arises for two reasons. First, with regard to the immigrant's marginality, most of the writers often overlooked or chose not to pay attention to the individual's marginality prior to his migration. Perhaps it is assumed that the immigrant prior to his migration was an integrated member of his own society. The assumption that the individual immigrant becomes marginal when he arrives in another country implies that he was a non-marginal member of his own country. The result is that, despite the long association of the concept of marginality with the study of immigrants, contemporary sociologists have failed to focus on the nature of societies from which individuals, especially Westernized professional individuals, migrate. Although some of the writers have acknowledged the marginality of the natives caused by Western penetration, there is almost no case study of the situation in which the native stranger, such as the Iranian professional, becomes an immigrant.

Second, most of the works dealing with marginality have concentrated attention on rural immigrants and members of minority groups. The concept of marginality has been defined largely in terms of intercultural and interpersonal conflict, and associated with the problems arising from the failure of acculturation and assimilation. Therefore, as far as I know, its possible applicability to the situation of middle class professional immigrant sojourners has not yet been examined.

This leads to the discussion of the concept of dual marginality which follows this discussion. With regard to the Iranian immigrants, it is my suggestion that the feeling of marginality or alienation in the home society coexists with the experience of marginality in this country. Therefore, I tend to propose that the older association of the immigrant's marginality with culture conflict in the host society must be linked to the marginal situation at home. Hopefully, this attempt will advance the application of the concept of marginality one more step.

Dual Marginality

It is my suggestion that, following the assumption of Park and Stonequist, one could conceive of dual marginality as a situation which is characterized by an extended marginality from one cultural setting to another. The concept of dual marginality is considered here as having two major components: native and alien marginality. Each culture produces a dual pattern of partial identification and divided loyalty for the individual. Thus dually marginal man is an immigrant who is a representative of marginality at home and abroad.

The dually marginal man in the restricted sense is an unintended immigrant who is not a fully integrated member of either society—home or host. Both situations, at home and abroad, contain for him some elements of uncertainty, non-belongingness, and insecurity. As a sojourber who has become an uncertain immigrant, he is caught between two conflicting reference groups in two different cultural settings.

In the case of the marginal man, there are two groups or two societies in which the individual feels marginal. But in the case of dually marginal man there are two societies representing not merely different but antagonistic cultures, and in each he holds a marginal position. Thus he sees himself in the midst of four social worlds, and is likely to experience a sense of marginality in any of these social worlds both at home and abroad.

The dually marginal man arises from cultural contacts resulting from colonization, Westernization, and intellectual migration. In some of the Third World countries the migration of their Westernized professionals has produced those kinds of marginal men—those who have become marginal both at home and abroad. The professional migration in the form of study abroad, as a process of self-estrangement is particularly conducive to this kind of marginality. It makes the individual uprooted both at home and abroad. Such dual marginality is almost a built-in definition of the situation itself, of being a middle class unintended immigrant. Even if the sojourner returns home, he is likely to experience such dual attachment or dual detachment. Nehru was an example of such a dually marginal man whose marginality resulted from Western penetration in Indian society. He expressed this feeling when he wrote:

> I have become a queer mixture of the East and West, out of place everywhere, at home nowhere...I can not get rid of either that past inheritance or my recent acquisitions. They are both part of me, and, though they help me in both the East and the West, they also create in me a feeling of spiritual loneliness not only in public activities but in life itself. I am a stranger and an alien in the West. I cannot be of it. But in my own country also, sometimes, I have an exile's feeling.[41]

A tragic but possibly over-generalized example of this duality of the Westernized individual in the developing countries is described by one of the Iranian social scientists as follows:

> A new man is born: the Western Oriental, an assembly-line product from the crucibles of imported culture. A heterogeneous, incomprehensible environment denies him any understanding of self; and rendered insecure by loss of his origins, his place in history, he has to construct a consciousness of self out of illusions. The more it eludes him, the more desperately does he struggle to get it, and the more he tries, the more unattainable it becomes. Finally, his only recourse is the display of an individuality, whose hollow interior he hopes to fill

> out with random bits of formal education, upper middle-class manners, and shoes that have [been] shined meticulously.[42]

However, it must be emphasized that when marginality at home resulting from delayed development (and its external and internal causes) leads to unwanted emigration, we would have an ideal situation for the development of dual marginality.[43]

The argument that we developed with regard to Iranian dual marginality may be sketched as follows: the Iranian undecided immigrant in this study experiences a situation of dual marginality. He is marginal to his own society as well as to the host society. His position is one of lack of stability in each. That is, he cannot relate himself in a constant way to his two or more reference groups in each country. He remains (up to a point) an uncertain immigrant in conflict about whether to adhere to American culture patterns and stay here or to embrace those of his own country and return home. As long as he remains an undecided immigrant, his situation may be characterized as one of dual marginality with a feeling of both belonging and not belonging to either society. While he has a feeling of being marginal at home, he experiences marginality in the United States. When psychologically he starts to organize himself as a permanent resident in this country, he is then a marginal man.

CHAPTER 2

Western Penetration

He (the marginal man) is an effect of imperialism, economic, political, and cultural.
Robert E. Park, 1937

To understand the dual marginality of the Iranian middle classes, who are the subject of this study, we need to know the broader historical processes of Western penetration in Iranian society. In other words, the social phenomenon of dual marginality of professional middle class immigrants has to be explained within the context of the interrelated, political, economic, and cultural impacts of Western imperialism upon Iranian society.

Thus the main objective of this chapter is first to provide a historical account of the general contact of Iran with the West, and second to explain the character of Iranian responses to Western political and cultural impositions.

A complete historical analysis of Western penetration in Iran is beyond the scope of this study. Only a separate study could hope to analyze adequately such a complex issue as the impact of Western imperialism upon the social structure of Iranian society. Instead, I concentrate on the historical processes of the Western impact as it has affected the Iranian social structure into which the foreign-educated, as the familiar stranger *(ashena-i-biganeh)* has emerged.

BACKGROUND OF CULTURAL CONTACT: An Overview

Up to the reestablishment of the Persian Empire under the Safavids (1500-1736) there was no significant cultural contact between Persia and the West.[1] The revival of religious-national spirit during the Safavid period coincided with major cross-cultural contacts. Shah Abbas (1587-1629) granted concessions to the British and the Dutch and thereby established some structural bases for international trade and diplomatic relations. But those Iranians who came directly in contact with the foreigners did not show an interest in their cultural perspective. Regarding Persian responses toward Western culture at this period, Professor F. Kazemzadeh writes:

> Those Iranians who came to have some knowledge of the West had little admiration for the "Franks." True, the Franks were masters at casting cannon, an art the Iranians hastened to learn; they were good at making pistols, watches, and pocket knives and sailing the seas. However, this did not make them superior in the eyes of the Iranians, who knew the Franks could contain the Turks in Central Europe only through coalitions, while Iran withstood them alone.[2]

There are, however, strong grounds for arguing a different case: namely, that it was because of the existence of "unity provided by the Shiite religion, and not due to any ancient racial characteristics, that there arose that extraordinary sense of self-sufficiency of nationalistic aloofness among Persians."[3]

IRANIAN RESPONSES: Acculturation and Conflict

What is perhaps striking is that the Iranians' contact with the West since the early eighteenth century has had a paradoxical dual character: on the one hand, a high degree of assimilation of Western ideas and values; on the other hand, an ongoing resentment both open and silent (symbolic reaction), toward the West.[4] Iran in this respect is particularly inviting to the student of a social process because one can see more clearly than elsewhere how two rather contradictory processes of acceptance or acculturation and resentment or conflict have coexisted. Obviously, such a historical character has some relevance for understanding of Iran's recent history. Moreover, it is this character which, as we will explain later, greatly influenced the forming of a peculiar social type, such as the familiar stranger, in contemporary Iranian society. Thus, in the following discussion I attempt to explain the processes of acculturation and conflict as they are manifested in the response of educated Iranians.[5]

Acculturation

By the early eighteenth century the Safavid rulership was replaced by Afghan domination, and Persia once more became a disintegrating nation without an effective central authority. In 1794 the Gajar dynasty was founded. It lasted more than one century, during which Iranian society fell victim to the ever-widening impact of Western Europe.

During this period increasing Anglo-Russian rivalry imposed a semi-colonial status upon Iran. Although it is true that Iran never fitted into the so-called classical pattern of a colony ruled by a foreign power, it nevertheless experienced Western influences that penetrated far beyond any of those that accompanied previous interventions.

It was during the nineteenth century that three major changes occurred in the power structure: the continuing rise of the power of the Ulama (Muslim theologians); the growing influences of foreign powers, especially Britain and Russia; and the rise of significant opposition to government and to foreign influence.[6] But it was the discovery of oil deposits in 1905 which brought about considerable foreign interferences and at the same time contributed to the already strong anti-foreign movement.

The first direct impact of the West on Iranian educational institutions came with the arrival of French and British military missions in the early part of the nineteenth century. Perhaps the most significant event at this time was the initiation of study abroad. It was following the humiliating major defeat by Russia (1813) that the process of study abroad began. Such humiliation resulted in a realization that Iran's weakness was due to its technologically backward army. Thus the first group of young Iranians was sent abroad to study military arts and techniques. "It was the Crown Prince Abbas Mirza who initiated the practice of sending students abroad, and it was his desire that they should study something of use to him, themselves, and their country.[7] By 1819 six of these foreign-educated Iranians returned home and were given vital positions in Iranian upper class ranks.[8] In addition to these repatriated Iranians, who were the first agents of Iranian Westernization, Persian newspapers also played an important role in introducing Western ideas. This was especially true in the case of those which were published abroad and sent to Iran. Among these radical newspapers one was *Ganun (The Law)* published by Malkum Khan in London.[9]

In 1921 a military coup d'etat by Reza Khan put an end to the Gajar dynasty and brought about a new era in Iranian history. In 1925 Reza Kahn made himself king (shah) and founded the Pahlavis.[10] Under Reza Shah's regime (1925-41) Iranian society experienced unprecedented changes at the cultural and societal levels. The sixteen years of Reza Shah's rule was a period of wholesale Westernization. But perhaps the most significant change, especially in relation to the present study, was the development of the core of a new middle class. Economic development and the centralization of authority produced a new social configuration in Iran. It was during this period that a system of public education was established. The number of primary and secondary schools rose from

432 and 33, respectively, in 1921 to 2,407 and 299 in 1941. In 1934 the University of Tehran was founded with a total enrollment of 886 students.[11] In order to meet the shortage of qualified personnel, more students were sent abroad. By 1938 about 400 of these students returned and were offered the highest positions available, regardless of their specific training and qualifications.

The repatriated individuals during 1930-50 displayed a wide range of values and ideologies; the predominant responses were either pro-Western or anti-Western capitalism. The pro-Western individuals, who were fascinated by advanced technology in Europe, returned home with a mission to build a "New Iran."[12] They proposed that Iranian society must become a follower society and detach itself from the past in order to become modernized (Europeanized). One of these individuals who later became a major political figure went far enough to say that "we must become Westernized from the feet to top of our head."[13] Some indication of this uncritical view of the West can be seen by the titles of the first foreign books which were translated into Farsi: *The Three Musketeers, The Count of Monte Cristo.*[14]

Despite such uncritical acculturation of the West, a more selective acculturation of the West against the West was also introduced by the foreign-educated Iranians of the late nineteenth and the early twentieth centuries.

Conflict

Having discussed the uncritical response of the early foreign-educated Iranians toward the West, I now turn to the Iranian anti-Western movements, which were also another response. We propose to discuss this aspect under two categories of "open resistance" and "silent resistance." By open resistance we mean the rise of oppositional movements against foreign domination since the end of the nineteenth century. The details of these movements prior to World War 2 have been discussed by others. With regard to the present study, I am primarily concerned with the existing ideological conflict of educated Iranians with the United States.[15]

The ideological conflict of the educated Iranian with the United States actually began after World War 2. Prior to World War 2 the Iranians' attitude toward America was positive. The positive image resulted primarily from the medical and educational services of private Americans in Iran. Bahman Niromand, an Iranian professor residing in Germany, in an angry anti-American book writes:

> The people liked these Americans very much because of their helpfulness. They built schools and equipped hospitals. They felt a sense of solidarity with the Iranian people in many respects. An American teacher took an active part and lost his life in the revolutionary struggles at the beginning of this century: in fact, the support given the revolution in the reports of the American press made a profound impression on the people and awakened a sympathy for America that continued to grow as the people became increasingly disillusioned with Britain.[16]

But this friendly aspect of Iranian-American contact was radically changed in 1946, once the United States' preeminence in the Western world was established. Iran, because of her geographical location and her vast amount of oil, was already the target of the major powers, including the Soviet Union. During the two years struggle over the nationalization of Iran's oil, the United States became involved in the Iranian politico-economic scene.[17] Thus the United States, instead of remaining as a third disinterested power, took an active role against the Iranian anti-imperialist movement.[18] The 1953 coup d'etat and the removal of Mossaddeq, whose philosophy was liberal, democratic, and nationalist, intensified Iranian hostility toward the United States.

With regard to anti-American feeling in the 1950s, the very same period in which the majority of the Iranians in the United States were politically involved in Iran, Daniel Lerner writes:

> It is the U.S. policy, not the American nation, that draws fire. But the feeling is intense and underpinned by a sense of deception. American performance has somehow not squared with Iranian expectations: it has not fulfilled its promises, she does not do what she says.[19]

From the 1950s to the present time (1977), Iranians regardless of their political orientation have interpreted American policy as a reflection of capitalist interests. Therefore, they regard their existing illegitimate political system as a creation of American and British imperialism.

Silent Resistance

The term silent resistance refers to the unique response of the Iranians to the oppressive situation imposed by external pressures or native marginality and alienation. Thus, in the following discussion, I shall explain the mechanism of covert reaction by the Iranian toward his past and his continuing oppressive and unpredictable situation. This discussion is necessary because the cultural baggage of the Iranian immigrants in the United States still contains some of these cultural systems.

The concepts of Persian individualism, escapism, basic insecurity, cynicism and distrust, mysticism, negativism, and emotionalism, to name a few, are central topics of the social scientists, Iranian and foreigners alike, who have addressed themselves to Iranian social psychology.[20]

We believe that the oppressive experience of Iranians in their past is of crucial significance in analyzing their pattern of behavior. This experience must be viewed not merely as one which had an impact on the attitudes of the individual. Rather, it must be approached as a historical process which produced a value system. As Iranian history indicates, Iranians have experienced a historical continuity of oppressive situations: long centuries of oriental despotism, tribal rivalries, Sunni-Shiite division, feudalism, and foreign dominations both direct and indirect from East and West.[21] This experience greatly influenced the self image of the Iranian individual and reinforced his need for privatism and covert resistance. If one views Iranian history in the light of this experience, it is possible to understand its manifestations on Iranian behavioral patterns.

It is true that throughout such experiences Iran has survived, and we are told that Iranians have been able to maintain the essential elements of their cultural tradition. That is, in relation to alien cultures, Iranians have been capable of acculturating without being assimilated or overwhelmed. In some cases, by working from the inside of the foreign dominating system, they were able to influence its administrative system and conquer the conqueror. Thus, while there were positive responses by Iranians toward external challenges, there is another dimension to their responses, which is manifested in the "symbolic reactions" of their culture.

In contrast to other perspectives, we tend to envisage these cultural systems as they are perceived by the Iranian himself in his social life. It is my suggestion that a sociological explanation of such perceptions can be derived from an application of a games model as recently formulated in *A Sociology of the Absurd:*

> The game framework is a model of behavior of man under consciously problematic situations trying to make sense of and plans for that and future situations of a similar nature.

> The model suggests the contextual establishment of identities, the situation-oriented aliveness to objects and events, and the calculation of strategies.
>
> . . . .
>
> The game model may not be suited to the analysis of all behavior, but rather to those situations having the properties of games—namely, imagination of the interactant's identities, motives, and strategies, and the development of counter-strategies, contingency tactics, and rescue operations.[22]

Having taken into account the Iranian historical experience, which is characterized by invasions and dominations, despotisms, deception, broken promises, and a pattern of domination and subordination, it appears that the games model is most fruitful for exploring some of the Iranian cultural qualities. The use of this model may not only make Iranian behavior intelligible, but it also helps us to understand the Iranian's conception of the world.

The Iranian has learned to believe that his world is a contest and in Camus's words "cannot be explained by reasoning."[23] To the Iranian this life "resembles a game of hazard where incalculable chances, good and bad, emerge and disappear, like bubbles on the surface of the water."[24] William Haas states:

> Nowhere, perhaps, on the earth has transiency been so deeply impressed upon the mind as in Iran since the collapse of the Sassanian Empire. The rise and fall of dynasties, the sudden changes from glory and wealth to utter misery, the springing up of cities and palaces where others had fallen in ruins, and the general uncertainty of individual fate warned that the present, whatever its appearance, is but an illusion. Nowhere, perhaps, has this feeling found an expression so powerful and at the same time so beautiful as in Iran, where poetical art, philosophical thought, and mystical experience combined to give it shape and thereby to free the soul.[25]

Therefore, as a result of such experience, the Iranians have developed the following "cultural systems" to play their game of life.

Ketman, or *tagiyyeh,* literally means dissimulation and concealment of faith.[26] The peculiar custom of *ketman* can be traced back to the early centuries of Islam. Its practice as a self-defense mechanism permitted an Iranian Shiite, in danger because of his religious belief, to pretend that he is a Sunni, a Christian, whichever best served his need of self-protection. According to this belief, it is not only permissible but also quite legitimate for a Shiite to conceal his faith. In the course of Iranian socio-political experience, this belief was reinforced, and its practice extended beyond religion. As a mask it serves to protect the individual against outside threat. It must be noted, however, that for an Iranian *ketman* is more than putting up a false front: it is a means to achieve psychological security and to "keep face."

The Iranian value system does not condemn the practice of *ketman* in everyday life. When the individual cannot take anything for granted, he takes refuge in *ketman.*[27] Its practice helps the individual to change his presentation of self to the conditions of time and space. Through *ketman,* in almost any situation in which he finds himself, he is faced with alternative courses of action. Thus the individual feels free to choose any course of action which is likely to be advantageous to him.

From the Iranian's point of view the practice of *ketman* is not considered hypocritical or immoral. It is the most logical reaction to his existential situation. When he faces an arbitrary suppressive situation, he uses *ketman* as a means to check the oppressor and protect himself. The supreme Iranian moralist, Sáadi, wrote, "A lie that brings good will is better than a truth which has malicious intent."[28] With regard to the practice of *ketman* in the face of political authority, Sáadi also wrote: "To urge a view against the Sultan's views is to surrender hope of living too: If he should say the very day is night, Say, "Lo, the moon, and there the Pleiads bright."[29]

Thus, when the individual's right is not built on a contractual basis, he has no choice except to misrepresent himself in order to survive. It is in this respect that *ketman* appears to be "a marvelous gift" possessed by the oppressed'[30] A Persian aphorism says: "If you do not want to be disgraced, adjust your conduct to the spirit of time and place.' Therefore, in his social relations the individual will act upon his definition of situation. If he defines it as hostile or suspicious, he avoids the conflict by wearing his mask.[31] Erving Goffman points out the same thing when he says: "In everyday life it is usually possible for the performer to create intentionally almost any kind of false impression without putting himself in the indefensible position of having told a clear-cut lie."[32]

Persian Individualism

Individualism functions as a license to maintain the individual's interest against external threats. The conspicuous individualistic tendency of the Iranian results from the way he perceives his world.

To him his world consists of individuals whose immediate interests are self-interest and self-protection. When it is assumed that everybody must be responsible for himself, then it is quite logical for individuals not to commit themselves beyond their interests. The individual simply has no conception of community or solidarity. He conceives of himself as a lonely person and thus, by emphasizing his individuality, he makes sense of his nonsense world.

Social commitment preassumes the protection of the individual's right and integrity. If society fails to safeguard an individual's right, then it is necessary for him to protect himself through cynicism and individualism. Therefore, outside the safety of the family, life seems insecure and often dangerous.

Iranian cynicism and distrust must also be understood in this light. The Iranian individual views life as a game, a contest where everybody constantly has to fight for his survival. This conception of life militates against a feeling of mutual trust and interdependence. Professor Lerner writes: "In a land habituated to define itself in terms of those outside powers which, at any given moment, threaten or protect it, there develops a chronic instability."[33] Thus it is this experience of insecurity which results in distrust and suspicion. "Consequently, in any group action, betrayal or at least fear of betrayal becomes commonplace."[34] Iranians believe that as long as no basis for altruistic trust exists, we can but respond accordingly to protect ourselves. "If I am trustful, I will only be taken advantage of by others."[35] "Do not trust even your eyes," is another Iranian saying. Thus, under such circumstances, individualism, mistrust, cynicism, and *ketman* become valuable assets in the struggle for existence. Despite the fact that Iranian culture essentially places high value on sincerity, concern for others, self-sacrifice, self-renunciation, and frankness, the individual finds it difficult to follow these standards. Under such ambivalent situations the Iranian drags out his life as best he can.[36]

FOREIGN EDUCATION AND EMERGENCE OF THE FAMILIAR STRANGER

Analysis of the modem Iranian social structure, notably the new middle class, has been done by other social scientists.[37] Here the concern is primarily with the expansion of the foreign-educated Iranian and the emergence of a social type such as the familiar stranger.

The past two decades in Iran have seen socio-economic changes whose main goal was the weakening of feudalism's hold on the social structure. Since the early 1960s unprecedented, rapid, uneven development has been taking place. The implementation of various reforms, especially land reform and the expansion of educational institutions, the rapid increase in oil revenues, and foreign capital investment, created a basis for the formation of a kind of dependent capitalism in Iran. One of the consequences of all these Western-imposed reforms was the expansion of the new middle class; closely linked with it was the rapid growth of foreign-educated Iranians.[38]

In 1950 the number of students abroad was 3,500; in 1964 this figure arose to 19,500. In 1972 a further 50,000 students were believed to be studying abroad.[39] It has been estimated that from 1957 to 1977 30,000 to 35,000 Iranian students came to the United States.[40] The number of university students in Iran also rose from 10,000 in 1953-54 to 67,000 in 1970, to 170,000 in 1976-77.

With regard to social composition, the present generation of foreign-educated Iranians represents a more heterogeneous group than the former generation. The majority of these individuals are from new middle class families. As a group, they are referred to as 'the professional bureaucratic-intelligentsia."[41] Individuals in this group are often the first in the history of their family to be educated abroad.

The newly foreign repatriated professionals and technocrats who became incorporated into the bureaucratic structure played an important role in the implementation of Western-directed reforms. In fact, they constituted the most active agents of the Iranian Westernization. Although the dichotomy of cultural identity versus Westernization was presenting a major conflict for Iranian intellectuals in general, for the most Westernized Iranians (*gharbzadeh,* meaning unauthentic Westernized) such a dichotomy was no longer experienced at the personal level. He had already departed from Iranian culture and its spiritual possibilities for modernization. That is, as a by-product of Westernization, he could no longer afford to deny his "structural assimilation." If, for the native intellectuals, Westernization meant "Westoxication," for the unauthentic Westernized individuals it meant a desirable process, full of promises and opportunities. Indeed, a great many personal and status interests were attached to their version of modernity.[42] To the extent that they remained unresponsive to the needs and values of the Iranian masses, in Karl Mannheim's words, they generally maintained "a help-yourself type of philosophy concerning society in general."[43]

In terms of power relationship, the foreign-educated Iranians, in general, essentially lacked political power. Therefore, as salaried professional people remained increasingly subordinate to the political authority but at the same time were bound together within their own professional groups and as individuals, they competed to strengthen their status interests. Perhaps the proper approach to their collectivity is by way of the concept of status community.

By status community we mean the larger group of repatriated Iranian professionals who identify themselves with their profession. Such a consensual community was institutionalized by the process of study abroad, and was increasingly expanded by the rapid development of the foreign-educated new middle classes. Therefore, both as a historical phenomenon and a social concept, the community has been closely connected with the larger process of Iranian Westernization.

The repatriated professionals as new elites within the strata of the middle class constitute a fairly well-defined and self-conscious interest group in Iranian society.[44] It is, in fact, a community within a community.[45] We call it a status community by virtue of the following characteristics:

1. Its members are bound by a sense of professional identity rather than class solidarity. That is, they are in contact with each other only by virtue of their membership.
2. Its members are organized into both formal and informal organizations through which they claim prestige and power.
3. Its members claim a high degree of superiority over the native-trained professionals in values and skills. Consequently, they enjoy a greater prestige.
4. Its members belong to a common sub-culture and share mobility aspirations, consumption norms, child-rearing practices, and leisure-time activities.
5. Its members, as the most Westernized Iranians, choose to limit their social contacts to their own status group. Among those who are the only foreign-educated members of their families, it is even difficult to reestablish intimate relationships with their own families.[46]

It must be noted, however, that the repatriated professionals by no means constitute a homogeneous or united group. They certainly lack the strength and self-dependency of the interest group in the United States. Therefore, as a group it is characterized by a major conflict between what we call the "old homecomers" and the "new homecomers." This conflict includes class disputes, as well as disagreements in the areas of professional standards and efficiency. For instance, with regard to a group of repatriated professionals, James Bill has identified four major types, such as the followers, the maneuverers, the technocrats, and the uprooters.[47]

The uprooter is the same type that we have called in a broader context the familiar stranger. He is a cultural hybrid whose divided identification stems from his over-resocialization abroad. The foreign education has also resulted, for certain individuals, in an upward mobility; thus, as socially detached individuals, they take an ambivalent orientation toward their own social biography and feel separated from their own families. When these individuals find themselves alienated from their own environment, the possible solution is emigration.

CHAPTER 3

Iranian Emigration

Pattern of Emigration

The Iranians do not have a long history of emigration.[1] Throughout Iranian history only one instance of relatively massive migration can be found. In the seventh century a large number of Persians migrated into India and formed the Parsi community.

Iranian professional migration began in the last twenty-five years with the institutionalization of study abroad of the new middle class. The Iranian immigrants in the United States are predominantly middle class, well-educated professionals, whose advent on the American scene—mainly in medical and higher educational institutions—is a comparatively recent phenomenon. They started to come to the United States around the 1950s often as temporary residents (students, interns) but eventually changed their status to permanent residents.

The annual report of the U.S. commissioner general of immigration lists 780 Iranian immigrants in the years 1925-32. However, as table 1 shows, starting in 1958 the Iranian immigrants admitted to the United States rose steadily and in 1968 exceeded 1,200 per year. The Iranian immigration began on a noticeable scale only in the early 1970s. From 1970 to 1973 another 10,000 were admitted as permanent residents. The commissioner's office estimates that total Iranian immigration into the United States from 1842 to 1976 amounts to about 34,000.

TABLE 1

Number of Iranians Admitted to the U.S.A. as Permanent Residents, 1953-75

Year of Entry	Status of Entry		Total
	Immigrant	Non-immigrant*	
1953	160	not available	
1958	433	139	572
1960	429	207	636
1963	705	408	1,113
1965	804	422	1,226
1968	1,280	825	2,105
1970	1,825	1,003	2,825
1971	2,411	1,317	3,728
1972	3,059	1,991	5,050
1973	2,998	1,915	4,913
1974	2,608	1,557	4,165
1975	2,337	1,147	3,484
TOTAL	19,049	10,731	29,817

SOURCE: Adapted from the Annual Report of the U.S. Immigration and Naturalization Service (1953-75).

*The category of non-immigrant applies to persons who had previously entered the United States with non-immigrant statuses like students, visitors, or businessmen and who changed their status to that of permanent resident.

NOTE: All U.S. Immigration and Naturalization Service data are for the fiscal year ending June 30 in the year indicated.

The pattern of Iranian migration does not involve "chain migration"; it is basically an individual migration. From a different perspective, it is, in fact, a problem of "brain drain"; that is, the migration of highly professional and technical Iranian people to the United States. For instance, from 1962 to 1969 Iran lost to America alone about 400 physicians and dentists and another 1,000 other professionals.[2] It is reported that there are more American-trained Iranian physicians in New York than in all Iran.[3] According to Iranian sources, approximately 70 percent of all the Iranian graduate medical students who come to the United States are not returning home; that is, the United States up to the early 1970s has absorbed into its medical structure over one-third of the graduates of Iranian medical schools.[4]

However, the Iranian migration of physicians is not essentially an "overflow." In the early 1970s an acute shortage of doctors in rural areas led the government to hire several hundred Pakistani physicians to work in the countryside. In 1973 there was only one doctor for every 4,000 Iranians (the ratio in the United States was one doctor for every 600 people). According to an official report in 1973, it cost $40,000 to $70,000 a year to educate a medical student in Iran.[5] The supreme irony is that the Iranian government through migration of her physicians alone used to pay annually $700,000 in "foreign aid" to the United States.

MARGINALITY AND EMIGRATION

A current fallacy is that brains go where money is. The fact is that the migration of professional Iranians is not basically a result of economic hardship. In the last twenty-five years many thousands of educated Iranians have migrated, despite opportunities, status recognition, and high salaries. These Iranians have chosen migration as an outlet for their general alienation from the socio-political system. Therefore, the Iranian migration as a voluntary action contains some essentially "involuntary" factors. Moreover, the migration of most educated Iranians involves also a process of becoming immigrants while they are studying abroad. Such a process involves resocialization and redefinition of goals and commitments. But for all educated Iranians, both students abroad and repatriated Iranians, a combination of political, social, and professional considerations tends to produce a "vocabulary of motive" for their non-returning or migration. That is, for foreign-educated Iranians in general the situation at home seems to involve at least three major dimensions of political, social, and professional marginality.

Political Marginality

The roots of political marginality of the new middle class, as a whole, lie in the great postwar crisis in Iran. This was a crucial period in which Iranian society was suffering from inner strains and external pressures. Furthermore, it was during this period that the new middle class as an emerging group came to realize that there was no room for all of them that some will be "in" and some will be "out"[6]; hence the discontent and frustration that arose from the conflict between well-founded aspirations and actual political opportunities.

Discussing the same period (the early 1950s), Daniel Lemer considers the elite marginality as a result of lack of participation in institutional structures of the Iranian political system. He particularly attributes the educated Iranian's marginality to his political alienation. He writes, "Counter-elite typically dissociate themselves from the governing elite and its institutions."[7] Since we are dealing with the same generation of Iranians as Lerner, we may assume that such political marginality of this group still remains in their middle class conception of political participation in a society where only a small group of elites are called into the sphere of participation. This is particularly true in the case of Iranians in this country who tend to think that, if they return, they will find themselves incapable of strengthening themselves politically as a group through their own initiative and resources. Crucial to an understanding of such situations is the fact that the political arena is viewed by the immigrant as the major source of his or her potential employment in Iran. Therefore the immigrant's understanding is that once returned he may find himself outside the governing elite or the political system, into which he must be reabsorbed or against which he must stand. If he accepts the effectiveness and legitimacy of the political system, he obviously compromises his political ideas and becomes reintegrated into the system.[8] Otherwise, he will either remain an outsider and refuse to become easily maneuverable by those of higher status and greater power, or eventually leave home and reside abroad.[9]

Social Marginality

While the political marginality of the foreign-educated Iranian may have followed rather than resulted from his foreign education, his social marginality stems basically from his resocialization abroad. In other words, it is a consequence of his over-stay abroad and his internalization of the Western value system. As a repatriated person who has been attracted by "modern thought," he finds himself to be a stranger in a social milieu which is thought to be "traditional" or at least different. Thus in his social life he may feel alienated and incapable of reestablishing extensive and ultimate interpersonal relations even with his closest friends and associates or his "welcomers."

In relation to the rest of the population, especially the native-educated countrymen, he may find himself in a situation of mutual rejection. He usually rejects his erstwhile compatriots because they do not share his "universe of discourse" or they do not respect his new-found value system. At the same time he is rejected and even stigmatized by others who view him as "Americanized" and as an alien to their own value system. Thus, paradoxically, he feels not at home with himself and finds himself a stranger among his own people. He even has no intimate sharing of values with some members of the ruling elite whose mode of life, because of uncritical acceptance of Western values, is more Western than his own. Therefore, if he decides to stay at home, he will probably seek integration into the sub-community of foreign-educated Iranians and continue to live isolated socially from the larger society.[10]

Professional Marginality[11]

Professional marginality is another dimension of some of the foreign-returned Iranian's dislocation. This form of marginality is caused by the conflict between his Western training and Iranian conditions. Once he returns, the American-trained professional, who has become accustomed to a different set of professional standards, no longer can approve the rigid scheme of things accepted in Iran. Thus his frustration stems from his inability to pursue his profession rationally, efficiently, and creatively.[12]

To be more specific, professional marginality of the returnee lies in the conflict between the ruling elite with its "old" training and the would-be elite with a more advanced knowledge. As professionals, both are striving for the recognition and economic security that ought to go with middle class existence. Referring to alienated elites in general, Daniel Lerner argues that "they oppose the current system not because they have no stake in it but because, on a range of social values, they want more than they get."[13] Therefore, if the returnee refuses to accept the pattern of polarities that reportedly dominate Iranian bureaucratic structures as well as Iranian society, he is likely to become an "uprooter," as described by James Bill.[14] According to him, "the Uprooter is competent, courageous, and non-corrupt (although he may be corruptible)...His goal is to transform the web itself and he will stand and fight for what he believes in...The Uprooter favors decisions based on merit rather than influence."[15]

It may be useful to present now, by way of illustration, the professional marginality of a "typical" American-trained returnee. For instance, to the doctor who has residency and practicing experience in American medical institutions, the existing Iranian medical system seems incompatible with his training. He has worked with the latest equipment in an advanced professional climate and has dealt with a literate if not educated body of patients. Now at home, the lack of proper facilities, especially in rural areas and small cities, the existence of a highly centralized administration, jealousy of the well-established professional, and the system of particularistic treatment (although he himself demands special treatment) will make it difficult for him to maintain his loyalty to his profession.

Furthermore, as an American-trained professional whose training in this country may have taught him to advocate academic freedom and professional growth, he may find himself suppressed by a system which he thinks limits his growth and undermines his academic freedom. Consequently, he may fail in readjustment and find no alternative except to detach himself from his professional commitment or to leave his country altogether.

PART II

A Case Study of the Iranian Community in the United States 1972–1978

CHAPTER 4

Types of Iranian Immigrant

General Characteristics of Sample

In this part I present a general picture of the demographic and social aspects of the members of the study. This is aimed to provide a concrete basis for further analysis in the following pages.

Population and Sex Distribution

Immigrants who participated in this study numbered 105. There were 70 persons from the New York State area, 27 from New Jersey and 8 from Pennsylvania. Of the 105 participants, there were 30 females.

Occupational Aspects

The professional distribution of the interviewees reveals that over 50 percent are in medical professions. This figure reflects the fact that Iranian professionals in the United States are overrepresented by physicians. This of course does not represent the Iranian professionals at home, for there is only one doctor for every 4,000 Iranians. A recent study reveals that the United States has approximately one Iranian medical graduate for every five at home.[1]

In terms of training and specialty, with three exceptions, physicians in this sample have had their medical training at home and their specialty in American medical institutions. Their specialties include pediatrics, anesthesia, obstetrics, psychiatry, surgery, and (in two cases) plastic surgery. The length of training for these specialties ranged from three to five years. Of the total population of physicians in this sample, 20 percent of the male doctors, including one dentist, are licensed physicians.[2] Among the female doctors there are two practicing physicians, both married to American doctors. With regard to their specialties, female doctors are overrepresented in anesthesia. This perhaps has to do with the fact that this specialty requires a shorter period of training.

TABLE 2

General Characteristics of 105 Respondents

Profession	Number
Physician	58
College Professor	10
Engineer	14
Nurse (R.N.)	23
Sex	
Male	75
Female*	30
Age	
Under 30 years	18
30-35 years	64
35-45 years	22

*This figure includes 23 nurses and 7 doctors.

Of the 30 females, 23 are nurses. They all had their college training at home but took additional courses and training in order to obtain permission to work in American hospitals. Three are supervisors, two head nurses, and the rest are working in operating rooms. It was found that most of the Iranian nurses prefer to work in surgical areas rather than in other wards, because of language problems and cultural differences. In the operating room there is a minimum of verbal communication and less chance of face-to-face interactions with the patients.

Iranian Ph.Ds constitute over 10 percent of the sample. With one exception, all have teaching positions in colleges and universities. There are five professors, six associate professors, and five assistant professors. Their fields of teaching include economics, chemistry, physics, statistics, and mathematics.

Age Distribution

The age distribution of sample members reveals that 58 percent of the interviewees are over thirty years of age.[3] This suggests that Iranian professional immigrants in this country are among the first generation of the new middle class who grew up in the last thirty-five years, in which personal involvement with the national crisis was profound. This period was a crucial one in Iranian history, in relation to both an internal crisis and the reconstruction of the Iranian image toward the Americans.[4]

Marital Status

Iranian migration, as indicated earlier, is basically an individual migration; the graduates usually come to this country in their late twenties and early thirties. It was found that over 60 percent of the interviewees came to the United States at age twenty-seven or older. This is consistent with Baldwin's findings.[5]

As to marital status, the Iranian immigrants usually come single and then either marry in this country or after a few years make a trip home and return with wives. Table 3 shows that 68 percent are married; out of this number, only 10 were married when they arrived here. Out of 68 married individuals 30 persons are married to non-Iranians. Among this group, males are overrepresented.

The unmarried interviewees, especially the males, expressed an unqualified preference for an Iranian mate. The reasons given for such preference were varied. Some interviewees pointed out the basic differences between Iranian and American cultures. Several reported that since they plan to return home, they prefer to marry an Iranian. Significantly, over 50 percent of the sample reported

TABLE 3

Marital and Immigration Status of 105 Respondents

Marital Status	*Number*
Married	68
Single	34
Divorced	3
Types of Marriage	
Married to Iranian women	24
Married to non-Iranian women	36
Married to non-Iranian men	3
Immigration Status	
Permanent resident	99
U.S. Citizen	6
Initial Visa	
Student Visa	32
Exchange Visa	63
Permanent Immigrant Visa	10

they had friends who were married to Americans and returned home, but whose marriages ended in divorce.

Despite these unfavorable attitudes toward marrying an American, the table above shows a relatively high rate of intermarriage among the Iranians represented in this sample. This is a manifestation of the high assimilating tendency of Iranians toward foreign cultures. Moreover, it reflects the fact that the population of Iranian females in the United States does not match the male population.

Immigration Status

In terms of status, as table 3 evidences, 99 members of the sample are officially permanent immigrants. Of 105 interviewees only 10 persons came to this country with permanent resident visas. The rest of them came with either a student visa (F-1) or an exchange visa. Among the immigrants, physicians mostly came to the United States with exchange visitor's visas. Those with the J visa are supposed to leave the United States when their training has been completed. Doctors with J visas are permitted to stay in this country for a five-year period.

It was found that those who initially came with exchange visitor's visas changed to permanent resident's visas either through marriage with an American or by leaving the United States for two years.[6] Some who were unable to obtain waivers for changing their visa went to Canada, where they could wait for reentry as permanent immigrants to this country.[7]

With regard to U.S. Citizenship, only six individuals admitted that they have become U.S. citizens.[8] But all permanent immigrants added that they have become permanent immigrants for practical purposes (job requirement) rather than becoming citizens of the United States. It is important to note that none of the U.S. citizens in this sample has yet participated in any local or presidential elections.

Social Biography

As for class origins, as table 4 shows, the majority of the respondents are from middle class families. Two broad categories account for over 90 percent of the groups: traditional bourgeoisie and professional non-bourgeois middle classes. This figure evidences that one of the distinctive characteristics of the Iranian migration is its middle class character. This finding is also consistent with two previous findings on the Iranian students in the United States. For example Borhanmanesh's study reveals that 8 percent of the Iranian students are from the upper class, 39 percent from the "upper middle class," 37 percent from the middle class, and finally 16 percent from the "lower-middle class."[9] In another study, Valipour found that the majority of the students are from dominant or middle class families.[10] It is significant to note that these surveys were mainly focused on undergraduate students rather than graduate students and professionals. Among the undergraduates, medical students and nurses were not presented because the majority of Iranian physicians have had their basic medical training in Iran. What is significant, according to the present finding, is that, for the first time, working class families have achieved a slight representation among Iranians educated in the United States.

TABLE 4

Socio-Economic Background of Sample Members

Upper Class*	3
Traditional middle class†	36
New Middle class††	56
Religious strata	6
Working class	4

*Includes the offspring of landowners, top of officials, cabinet members and army officers
†This category includes those who are self-employed, such as *Bazari* (merchants).
††Includes the offspring of *karmandan* (government employees) and private employees. The members of this class are engaged in professional, technical, cultural, and administrative occupations and are by and large a salaried middle class.

In terms of father's occupation, over 50 percent are sons and daughters of *karmandan* (government employees), about 36 percent are the offspring of *bazari* (merchants), 3 percent of former landowners, former cabinet members, and army generals, and another 10 percent working class families and *ulama* (clergy).

Religious Affiliation

In religious affiliation, 96 are Shiites, 2 are Christians (Armenians), 2 are Bahais, and 5 are Jewish. It is significant to point out that while Armenians emphasize their distinctive nationality and participate mainly within their own Armenian-American community, the Jewish Iranians in this sample displayed a strong identification with Iran rather than with Israel or the Jewish community in the United States.

It seems that the Jewish identification with Iran is rooted in the history of the Iranian-Jewish contact initiated by Cyrus the Great. The beginning of this identification seems to have occurred when "in addressing Persian officials, the Jewish leaders readily designated their own God as the 'God of Heaven,' making him appear almost identical with the Persian Ahuramazda."[11]

THE IMMIGRANTS' RESPONSE

With regard to questions such as "Do you intend to settle in the United States?" "Would you encourage Iranian students to remain in the U.S.?" and "How do you define your present situation, as a settler *(mandegar)* or as a would-be returnee?" it was found that out of 105 respondents 85 individuals defined their situation as "temporary" residents, with no definite plan at the present time. Most important, among the so-called undecided immigrants 15 individuals had at least once returned to Iran but had remigrated to the United States. Respondents' reasons for remaining undecided immigrants were primarily "because of the situation in Iran," as many put it. Those who viewed their situation as settler gave two reasons for their decisions: the education of their children, and their own professional achievements in the United States.

Despite the fact that the majority of the respondents share a situation of uncertainty and ambivalence *(belataklif)*, they respond to it in certain different ways. The immigrants' response can be placed somewhat arbitrarily in four major overlapping types, each of which indicates a distinctive pattern of behavior. In this categorization we are concerned with relatively prevalent orientations; thus, if we make any generalization, it applies to the majority but not necessarily to all individuals—the concern is not so much with the particular individual as with the type he or she represents.[12]

The Iranian immigrants in this study, judging by the collected data, may be divided roughly into the following types, which are also known to the immigrants themselves:

1. Ambivalent *(belataklif)*
2. Settler, or Persian Yankee
3. Self-exile *(siyasi)*
4. Cosmopolitan

Ambivalent Iranian

The self-designation *belataklif* was often expressed by the majority of the respondents in this study. What they meant was that they were unable to choose between the two counties, Iran and the United States.

> I am really a "belataklif" person. Do not know what to do. While being an Iranian in my inmost self, I am nonetheless uncertain where I belong to.

or

> I have become a stranger in both countries. When I was in Iran I felt like a foreigner. Here I am an alien too.

The dominant orientation of this type of immigrant is a state of dual detachment accompanied by a sense of general estrangement. While they have a feeling of marginality at home, they are at the same time more conscious of their different form of marginality in the United States. Moreover, they are fully aware that their position in each country requires a special type of "sacrifice" and conformity, alienation and frustration, loss of ties and abandonment of hopes. However, they find themselves fully unprepared or unwilling to accept one and reject the other. As one informant put it:

> I am always aware of my non-belongingness in both countries. Nevertheless, I will some day make up my mind.

Another one said:

> Every time that I receive a letter from home, I begin to question why I am here. I always write back to my family and promise them that I will go home next summer.

The ambivalent type's mind is always preoccupied with the question of to go or not to go. But since he is closely in touch with two different groups who give him contradictory advice, he finds it difficult to make a definite decision. He has a reference group which consists of his friends who returned home and found themselves disappointed. Some of them stayed home and others returned here. He has also another reference group which includes those friends who feel they should have returned home and found themselves disappointed. Some of them stayed home and others returned here. He has also another reference group which includes those friends who feel they should have returned home but find it too late to do so. Obviously, both these groups generalize their own experiences and ask for support from others to confirm their own assertions. Thus the ambivalent Iranian has always the feeling that he might face the same situation that his friends in each group have faced. His feeling is represented in the following statement:

> We do not know what to do. It is almost three years that we are planning to return home. Each time we are going to pack up, we meet another Iranian who tells us not to return because he himself returned home, but came back here as a failure. We also have friends who tell us before you establish yourself, you better return home. They say it is too late for them to change their life.

A large proportion of the members of this group seems to be considering the idea of leaving this country, but since their state of mind is one of skepticism and uncertainty, accompanied by an earlier alienation from home, many are likely to remain here and join the settlers.

The more the Iranian remains in America as an undecided, uncertain immigrant, the less likely will he be to return, because, as time passes, he becomes more convinced that he cannot afford another readjustment. As one person stated:

> I should have returned home three years ago; not that I am more Americanized, now, but because I have already established myself in my present position.

Despite his well-established life, the ambivalent person lives in a constant state of tension and excessive self-consciousness. He is torn between a nostalgic love for what he left behind, accompanied by a strong guilt feeling, and a growing attachment toward what he has ahead in his present situation.

> I always tell my American friends that I am not an immigrant like other alien physicians. I never came with the intention of staying here. I am still uncertain what to do.

Another doctor described her feeling in the following words:

> I am afraid that some day I have to face the reality and make a final decision. I am very hopeful that I Will return home.

With regard to his cultural and social marginality here, the ambivalent Iranian, up to a certain point, remains extremely conscious of his cultural identity. As long as he remains an undecided person, the more he becomes Americanized, and the more he feels like an outsider. That is, his greater familiarity with American culture tends to make him more aware of his own cultural heritage.

> The longer I stay here, the more I feel I do not belong to this country. More and more I am concerned about not being Iranian enough.

> Sometimes I ask myself why I exiled myself. I believe most of my friends have a guilt feeling concerning their over-stay in this country.

However, there are indications that a decision to become a settler does not put an end to the individual's experience of dual marginality. Restlessness and ambivalence will continue to dominate his mind. For example, a practicing physician said:

> I have a friend who has almost everything he wanted to have: high income, two large cars, and an expensive house. But he always tells me that his heart and mind still reside in Iran. Emotionally, he still is not sure where he stands.

An Iranian social scientist described his feeling in this way:

> My problem is that I am highly aware of my cultural alienation in this country. Whenever I go to a party I have a constant feeling that I am apart from the people around me.

The immigrant's dissatisfaction with his present situation is a result of status inconsistency. That this type of person has no intention to readjust himself to his present environment. Therefore, his feeling of dissatisfaction cannot be explained only in terms of his inability to readjust.

Here are a few typical comments by this type of immigrant. A physician, who in the last two years has been thinking of going home, stated his uncertainty in the following terms:

> I stay in this country because I am not certain of readjustment at home. The horror of the return hangs constantly over my mind. Almost all of our friends here discourage us from returning home. *But we know that most of them are really dissatisfied with their present life.*

An outstanding surgeon, who believed that over-staying in this country had intensified his alienation from his home, had this to say:

> I urge every Iranian student in this country to return home right after the completion of his training. It is too late for me to go through another process of readjustment. *But I must admit that deep in my heart and at the back of my mind exists the feeling of disappointment.*

A female anesthetist described her dual marginality in the following statement:

> I must admit that I feel an alien both at home and here in this country. Last year I went home with the intention of staying there. Soon I realized that everything has changed, the Iran that I dreamed of just was not there. Everywhere I was a misunderstood person even my brother once called me a mentally ill person. So I decided to come back and live my isolated life. That is why I said at the beginning *that at home I was a native stranger, here I am a real foreigner.*

Another practicing physician who was highly disturbed about his present situation said:

> Despite the fact that I have resisted Americanization, I have a nagging feeling that I am not Persian enough. *After seven years of living and working in this country, I am still deeply troubled by the choice before me.*

An Iranian-American scientist who came to the United States in 1953 stated:

> Iranians are the most successful group in American society.

> They brought to the United States outstanding talents and professions, especially in science and medicine. They are highly regarded by Americans, yet their minds and hearts are constantly directed toward Iran. No matter how successful they have become in America, most Iranians have a feeling of not fully satisfied accomplishments. They love to return to Iran, but have not forgotten the circumstances that caused their emigration.

It would seem that the situations of the ambivalent Iranians are situations of what I have called dual marginality. The characteristic notes of their social situation are those of undecidedness and utter uncertainty, born of the awareness of marginality in both societies. They continue to experience this until they either become full-fledged members of their host society or return to Iran and readjust to the new situation.

The Settler, or Persian Yankee[13]

Iranians both at home and abroad use pejoratively the term *Americai Maab* for an Iranian who is too much Americanized. The Iranian community in this country regards this type of immigrant as an unauthentic Iranian, one who no longer represents the "perfect" type of Iranian. The term also implies that such an individual has lost himself and forgotten his cultural and national identity. The Iranian press and politicians go even further and call a Persian settler in this country a stateless person who has betrayed his people and instead is worshipping aliens.[14]

Regardless of how others would like to view a Persian Yankee, the fact is that he himself defines his status in this country as a Persian settler. That is, after a few years of living as an undecided immigrant, he finally has come to terms with his situation. As one states: "I finally could adjust myself to my unpredicted life."

The Persian settler represents a typical immigrant student who came here as a trainee, then became officially a permanent immigrant but remained for a few years as an undecided sojourner. Finally, after several trips back and forth, he chose this country as a place for his permanent settlement. Therefore, the settler's decision of permanent migration as an outlet for his discontent with Iranian society, is determined by his type of experience at home and in the host society.

The data show that about 20 percent of the respondents in this sample called themselves *mandegar* (settlers); that is, they defined their migration as permanent, not temporary. Although some of the so-called settlers did not rule out the possibility of return, such possibility to most of them seemed remote.

The settlers, as would be expected, are the older ones, and those who are married to non-Persians. They have school age children and are likely to own property in this country. Their life both public and private is determined more by American patterns than Persian standards.

The dominant orientation of this type of immigrant is his general alienation from Iranian society. The self-designation of *randeh va mandeh* implies that such an individual is already uprooted from home and is a *mandegar* (settler) in his present environment. Some might have experienced such alienation long before they left the native country. Others might have realized it when they returned home after a long period of living abroad.

Following are a few typical responses to the question, Why did you decide to come back to this country?

> I lived here seven years as an undecided Iranian. I had a good position as a pediatrician and had permission to reside in this country. For two years I hesitated whether to stay or return. I finally went home and lived there for one year. From the very first month I realized that I no longer belonged there. I was not a political man, but I became political because every issue or discussion could have political implications.

> If you want to live there, you must be like them. They (Iranian elites) know how to conduct their behavior. I could not compromise my values.

> It is true that I was given a higher position at home than in the United States, but the organization in which I was working did not permit me to exercise my full responsibility both as a professor and a citizen. By coming back to this country, I preferred more security and self-satisfaction at a lower social status and a life-time cultural alienation.

> I came back to the United States because I did not find myself at home. Everywhere I was a misunderstood person. It was my failure, because I failed to behave according to their expectations.

Evidence of class consciousness is also found among most of the individuals in this category.

> It was true that I was a foreign-educated Iranian but the fact was that I did not belong to "them."

> It was not enough to have a foreign degree, I needed to know someone from "first class" (upper class).

> The older foreign-returned Iranians who belong mostly to upper class families do not take us seriously.

The larger proportion of these informants expressed the belief that lack of connection or family ties resulted in their failure to adjust themselves to the Iranian job situation. Almost everybody believed that if he had proper connections he would have no difficulty in establishing himself. But these findings are inconsistent with two previous studies concerning non-returning Iranian students.[15]

With regard to readjustment to the Iranian situation, an unmarried female informant expressed her disillusionment in a different way. For example:

> I prefer the loneliness in this country to the lack of freedom at home. Here I am able to be myself, and I don't care what other people think of me.

One, discussing her frustrating experience at home said:

> I was constantly under pressure as to why I did not marry. Every day my parents would remind me that I am getting old and should marry.

Still another doctor who was critical of Iranians' attitude toward educated women stated:

> My colleagues both, men and women, could not accept me as what I was. They expected me to act as an old-fashioned Iranian woman.

A woman physician, who preferred the social anonymity of American life to living in male-dominated Iranian society, stated:

> After six years living in this country I went home to live a happier life among my family. But soon I realized that I have two conflicting situations; one as a "foreign-returned"

> woman and the other as a female American-trained doctor. To most of my friends I was a familiar stranger *(ashena-i biganeh)*. I just could not tolerate that situation, so I came back to this country.

Another woman informant described a frustrating experience encountered by many unmarried women when they return to Iran:

> Most of the people around me did not appreciate my personal achievements. They were more concerned about my personal life in the United States. Those who asked me to date them did not respect me as a Persian girl. Almost everybody believed that I was no longer a virgin. Even an American-trained man, who had divorced his American wife and wanted to marry me, wanted to know in advance if I was still a virgin. This was really insulting to me. That is why I like to stay here and live my own life.

As mentioned earlier, almost 9 percent of the respondents are members of Iranian minority groups. Although they define their migration as voluntary, it contains certain involuntary factors. This is especially true in the case of Bahai's, who according to the Iranian constitution are not permitted to hold any government jobs unless they conceal their religious affiliation. As one Baha'i nurse stated:

> ...after my training I returned home to serve my people. I became disappointed over the impossibility of making myself a useful member of my own community. I could not tolerate people's hostile attitude toward my family. It is true that by coming back here I could not get rid of my minority situation, but here at least I do not feel direct prejudice against me. If I live in Iran, no matter what I do, or how high a position I may attain, I and my family may be ruined at any time, by events beyond our control.

An Armenian woman doctor, who was attracted by the melting pot character of American society, stated:

> I prefer to be a member of the minority group in this country rather than to be a suppressed member of the Armenian community in Iran. In my small town in Iran my family are still viewed as unclean *(Nejes)* people by the Moslems. Here almost nobody cares about my religion. In Iran I am an unclean and unaccepted minority member, here I am just an alien.

As all these comments indicate, the settler has usually decided to become a permanent resident in this country not necessarily because of his love for American life but rather because of his dislike of the Iranian life. In other words, unlike most American immigrants, he is pushed away by home factors rather than pulled in by host factors.

Therefore, we conclude that the unwanted permanent migration of this type of immigrant is a reaction to his inability or unwillingness to readjust himself to his home situation. The fact that most of these respondents have at least once returned home further supports this assertion.

As a result of such frustrating experiences this type of immigrant is no longer an undecided immigrant. For him Iran is a burden laid down; it is something of the past. He is cut off from home realities by a deep-seated cynicism and mistrust.

With regard to the changes and events at home, he maintains the role of detached observer. He does not read Persian newspapers nor other materials sent to him. Several informants admitted that they get angry whenever they read a Persian newspaper, because "all are full of lies and distortions." As one notes, there is an overemphasis by the settler on the negative aspects of the Iranian situation rather than on improvements. This type of immigrant is still the prisoner of his self-image from the Iranian past and is not yet ready to forget. One hears, "I have paid the price of my national commitment." One expressed his detachment from Iran in the following words:

> America is my second home. Sometimes I think I have only a second home. I really feel detached from Persia. Yet my family at home worries about me.

Another person, who did not deny his cultural alienation, in this country, stated:

> I see little point in thinking and acting like a Persian, but that's what I am. And there is little need to try to be something else.

What is evident in these statements is that the commitment to the role of the national is giving way to an individual-centered identity. Furthermore, in this category we find the Persian Yankee who is also the bearer of "a secret marginality," of which David Riesman has written. The Persian Yankee is marginal to his marginality because he is conscious of his group identification but does not feel the group protest quite fits him.[16] He views himself as an integrated part of American society and insists that everyone treat him as such; but since he certainly is not an American, he is likely to remain marginal to his marginality. In other words, by insisting on his good adjustment in this country, he is trying to get rid of his cultural marginality and isolating himself from his own national community in this country.

Self-Exile *(siyasi)*

Only a few informants revealed their political orientation or considered themselves as involuntary political emigrants. However, there are indications that if one takes a random sample of the total population, there are a considerable number of self-admitted political emigrants.

The self-exiled Iranian immigrant is *siyasi* (political self-exile) who identifies himself with the political community of Iranians in this country. He makes no attempt to hide his political disagreement with the political system at home or in the host society.

Whether he is a professional or a lifetime student, this type of immigrant as an Iranian radical considers himself the most aware element of the immigrant community. He is always engaged in an attempt to prove to the host people that he has no personal desire to live here. Therefore, he presents ideological justification for his continued residence in this country. As one often hears:

> I cannot go back home because of my political view,

or

> I am a political refugee and have no choice except to stay here and wait.

Among his American friends the political immigrant has an intense desire to publicize himself as a victim of "American imperialism." With regard to the reason for his migration, he underestimates personal conflicts and overemphasizes the existing institutional conflicts at home. Therefore, he expects to be viewed as one who sacrifices his time, energy, professional goals, and even his freedom at home for the sake of principle—a Persian martyr.

The response of the political immigrants, when they were asked to explain how they found their present life, might be better appreciated in these comments: a physician who owns and operates a medical pavilion defined his situation in the following words:

> I consider myself as a political refugee. I am not able to return home under the present circumstances. If the political conditions were favorable for political opposition, I would undoubtedly return home. I belong to a generation whose revolution is arrested and has failed.

Another individual who was a former member of the Iranian political community stated:

> I am not an immigrant and I never considered this country as a place to settle down. For me American life is something transitory. I regard my present environment as an instrument of my nationalistic wishes.

The fact that the Persian political immigrant has chosen his "enemy" as his host and has taken refuge in the host society has created a peculiar situation which is rather unique. In terms of political disagreement with both political systems—at home and in the host country—the immigrant finds himself in a situation of dual political alienation.

A social scientist who is critical of both political systems—the system at home and the system in the United States—described his dual alienation with the following thoughts:

> ...whether I live here or at home, as a responsible intellectual I have the feeling of uneasiness and alienation. Under the present circumstances I do not have the feeling of belonging, sharing, or participating in either society. Here I live under a capitalist system which is somehow responsible for my uprootedness. How can I reconcile myself with this system?

Another informant framed his feelings in these words:

> When I came here I was deeply impressed by the ideas of Jefferson. But soon I realized that there is a difference between the American ideals and the American realities. Whenever I see the oil companies headquarters, they remind me of the injustice they have done to my people.

One of the informants, an American citizen, said:

> I am strongly against the foreign policy of the United States. It is true that I am a citizen, but I had to become a citizen in order to carry on my political activities as an Iranian-American.

As these comments indicate, the meaning that the political immigrant attaches to the American political system not only is to a large extent a reflection of Iranian-American historical relations but is also a by-product of the individual's political orientation.

In short, we may conclude that this type of immigrant as a result of his political conviction is experiencing a situation of conflict and marginality. For him the involuntary migration, although less damaging morally, is catastrophic intellectually. Because of such frustrating situations some have chosen to reconsider their political position and return home. Others are too doctrinaire to redefine their political thought and are determined to become *bastneshin* (taking refuge) and maintain the attitude of wait-and-see. With regard to their concern for Iranian society, the political immigrants, as the most critical elements of Iranian society, whether they stay here or return home, are each likely to remain—in Socrates' words—"a permanent alien, one who tends to question every form of government and any kind of reformation."[17]

The Committed Professional

This type of immigrant is usually a committed scientist or physician who considers himself a member of the international community and identifies himself more with his profession than with his nationality. In response to the question of identity, he ignores his social biography and calls himself "a citizen of the world." Instead of commitment to the role of the national, he maintains commitment to his profession and associates himself with the members of the world of academia.

With regard to his migration, he argues that he has a more "legitimate" reason than other groups. That is, he justifies his staying in this country in terms of his inability to exercise his Western professional standards at home. Here are some typical comments which illustrate this point.

An outstanding surgeon who has lived in this country for fifteen years stated:

> Most of my friends are staying here because the working conditions necessary for their talents do not yet exist at home.

A physician who viewed his situation from a professional perspective said:

> I am in love with my profession and am deeply engaged in research. For me the most significant factor is my professional

> responsibility. As a professional man I cannot live up to the difficulties that I will face in Iran.

Another informant, referring to his friends' experiences, stated:

> I know a few Iranians who were well-established in this country. They went home with the firm intention of staying there, but they came back because they faced many difficulties in exercising their professional duties.

It seems that this type of immigrant resembles the "uprooters," whose situation is described in James Bill's study "The Iranian Intelligentsia."

> The Uprooters struggling in the Pahlavi University web-system tend to possess an American undergraduate education through which they have acquired certain achievement values. In a sense, their entire existence and identity has become tied up with the skills and knowledge they have obtained through such an education. By their very existence in the system, they pose a threat to the traditional polarities and the Maneuverers who buttress such polarities.[18]

It is in relation to such situations that one of the doctors teaching at the medical school of Howard University writes:

> I would love to go back home, but those who are at the top are afraid to compete with the younger generation.[19]

Another physician, who is a resident at Georgetown University, also states:

> I believe every Iranian physician in this country wishes to go home to serve his people. In this country no matter what higher position we have, we are still aliens, and it is precisely this that hurts us. But I still prefer to live here as an alien and wonderer, because it is better to be an alien than a failure at home.[20]

As these comments suggest, the committed professional regards the implementation of his professional knowledge as of primary concern and more important than any other involvement or commitment. By living in this country, while he might have unsatisfied psychological needs, professionally he finds himself released from the restraints and constraints to which he might be subjected at home. Therefore, migration for this type of immigrant has produced a new situation in which he becomes to a certain degree a cosmopolitan. As a result of his physical detachment, he tends to fulfill his function as part of the professional world to which he belongs and to which he brings his special contribution. One immigrant states:

> I have no particular country. I live wherever I find my professional satisfaction. I am a psychiatrist and I need a healthy, free, and stimulating environment in order to perform my duties.

Obviously, an over-expression of individuality or "internationalism" is one of the marked features of migration affecting many individuals. The immigrant says he becomes an autonomous man, bound by no local attachment. However, we must point out that for this type of Persian immigrant migration has not fully liberated him from his conventional modes of thought and culture. In other words, because of his unwanted migration, he is not a stranger with an objective attitude as discussed by Simmel and Schutz. The loss of status, and his unwanted migration do not permit him either to remain an outsider or to be a real cosmopolitan.

Despite the fact that this type of immigrant apparently views himself as a committed professional and emphasizes professional achievements, if he is offered an influential position at home, even as an administrator, he is likely to ignore his academic responsibilities. As one of the well-informed respondents stated:

> Most of the Iranian scientists in this country are seeking high and influential positions. If one is a physician, he expects to be invited home as a minister of health or as president of one of the universities.

However, most of the individuals in this category deny having such high expectations and are willing to return if they are given a job corresponding to their specialty.

It is interesting to note that while this type of immigrant is especially critical of the "discriminating character" of the Iranian bureaucracy, he himself demands special treatment. That is, the American-trained professional, on the one hand, advocates treatment based on the universalistic criteria; but, on the other hand, he expects to be given power and prestige based on his particularistic quality. One often hears: "I expected to be treated as a man who has had a "better training" or "My superior had a native education, and I just could not accept his orders." Perhaps these complaints are justified when they are related to professional qualifications. But they seem unjustified when directed toward social treatment. Let me quote some of the complaints to illustrate the point.

One frustrated physician who came back to this country expressed the following feeling:

> I did not want to follow the rules; when I went to the officials, I did not bow and I did sit down without permission to do so. I had no reason to do what others were willing to do. As a result of this behavior, they became angry at me and this complicated my situation. So, I decided to leave the country.

Another person who did not want to be inspected at the customs in the Tehran airport said:

> The officer did not believe me when I said all I have are books and nothing else. I told him I am returning home to serve my country and these books are my only valuable things. He told me, "Who invited you to come back? Go back wherever you were."

The same individual added:

> I just could not stand the behavior of people. They do not take you seriously. Every time you have a conversation with an official, it is likely to be interrupted by a newcomer. When you ask an address, the officer on the street does not give an answer. People on the street and in the bus push you without apologizing. If you say anything to them about your experience in America, they laugh at you.

Despite the fact that this type of immigrant maintains that his motivations for staying here are altruistic and professional, there is some evidence to indicate that these motivations are more sociopolitical than merely professional. However, we must point out that for those individuals who identify themselves with the world of academia, such new identification seems to be a means by which they can get around their national marginality and integrate themselves into a new collectivity. Therefore, as a type of cosmopolitan person the committed professional has become an individual with wider horizons and a more detached and rational outlook.

CHAPTER 5

The Immigrant Without a Community

The general purpose of this chapter is to present an analysis of the nature of community and in-group relations as displayed by the Iranian immigrants. First, I will attempt to identify the particular features of the community as well as the immigrants' communal relationships. Second, I will explain certain structural strains which are superimposed upon the community and control the immigrant's in-group relationships.

THE ETHNIC COLONY

"Colony" as it is conceived here refers to a kind of distinguishable residential area; that is, a distinctive ethnic locality. It seems that the ethnic settlements in the United States had their origin mainly in the arrival of the first generation of rural and non-skilled immigrants of the nineteenth century. As a consequence of chain migration, immigrants tended to settle in the same neighborhood with other immigrants of their own nationality.[1] Thus the ethnic settlement emerged as a center for reconstruction of a new network of social interactions between relatives and friends from the same country. As Don Martindale maintains, the tendency for ethnic enclaves to come into existence was partly an outcome of this dependency upon close relatives and friends in the early stages of the migration process.[2]

The primary function of the immigrant settlements as zones of transition was to facilitate the survival and readjustment of the immigrants in their minority situation. Stonequist noted that the immigrant colony in America is a bridge of transition from the old world into the new; a halfway house on the road of assimilation.[3] Thus the alienation and uprooting of the immigrants led to the formation of ethnic enclaves to preserve the familiarity of rural life and to meet the needs of minority status.[4] Furthermore, in the face of a dominant group, the ethnic community as a territorial identity was sought to provide ethnic legitimacy for its members in an alien and hostile environment.[5]

However, according to most of the recent studies on ethnic groups in America, immigrant settlements tended to be a one or two-generation phenomenon. This implies that as a result of social mobility the second generation of non-racial immigrants has been able to move up and out. This of course does not mean that, for those below the upper middle class, membership in ethnic groups has lost its significance. The same studies have found that ethnic and religious groupings are still decisive in residential patterning. It is at the higher social class levels that that group allegiance and identification have shifted from ethnic ties to cohesiveness within professions and work organizations.[6] In relation to present-day ethnic settlements, Maurice Stein maintains that "there is some evidence that present-day areas of third settlements display only a minimum of distinctive ethnic patterns, with the life style of the community being mainly class-determined."[7] This implies that ethnic colonies in the United States have become peripheral and are no longer able to fulfill the needs of a minority group.

With regard to the sociology of the ethnic community, it is evident that classical sociological assumptions about the ethnic neighborhood were based mainly on the immigrants' character and on existing conditions in the United States in the nineteenth century. These assumptions about ethnic settlement formation seem today no longer appropriate in describing the mode of settlement of professional immigrants in this country. Both the pattern of migration as well as the receiving society, in this case the United States, have undergone substantial changes. Thus new circumstances seem to call for different explanations, not only for the immigrants' settlement but also for their assimilation into the larger society.

The alien professional who comes to the United States today represents a new type of immigrant with higher qualifications. He enters a substantially different setting in which a multiplicity of loyalties and dual citizenship are no longer hard to maintain. Moreover, as a qualified professional he is welcomed by the host and is permitted to remain a mobile individual with no immediate demand for his permanent settlement in any given place.

As for the immigrant's status, he possesses a transplantable profession, an urban life experience, and greater familiarity with a *Gesellschaft* type of society. In some cases, as a result of Westernization of his home society, he is Americanized in his own country before he comes to America. In terms of his professional choice and his residential pattern, he resembles more a member of second and third generation American-born immigrants rather than of first generation immigrants.

Since there are immigrant professionals from many countries in the U.S. with distinctive racial and professional characteristics, each case requires special examination. The following discussion will present an explanation of the prevailing residential pattern of the first generation of Iranian immigrants. It must be remembered that, since there is no record of their numbers, I shall rely exclusively on the sample of this present survey.

It is found that the immigrants who are the subject of this study live with no distinguishable pattern of common locale. By a common locale I mean a relatively heavy concentration of immigrants similar to that of Little Italy, the Arab neighborhood, and Cuba in Exile. In this sense a "Little Iran" is almost non-existent. Almost none of the informants identified his residential area as a Persian section or block. The existence of an Iranian locality was unknown to all the immigrants. When the informants were asked how they chose their residential area, almost every one answered it was done on the basis of occupational considerations and desirability of the area. When they were asked if they knew of other Iranian families in their neighborhood, 80 percent of the respondents who had lived over a five-year period in the same neighborhood did not know more than two other Iranians in their area. In short, the prevailing residential settlement of the respondents in this survey has almost no ethnic overtones and more resembles that of American professionals rather than any ethnic group.

WHY LITTLE IRAN DOES NOT EXIST

Little Iran does not exist, for the same reasons that the traditional ethnic settlements no longer exist for the second and third generation of other immigrants. The Iranians arrived in this country at a time when the host society had already undergone a rapid urbanization process and the disintegration of distinctively ethnic institutions. Moreover, Iranians' pattern of migration as well as their social conditions are hardly conducive to the formation of collective settlement.

First, the pattern of Iranian migration does not involve chain migration. It is not basically a family migration. Eighty percent of the immigrants in this survey arrived in this country as the sole member of their families. The majority of the informants came as unmarried individuals. Furthermore, the Iranian immigrant professional is usually a student immigrant—a sojourner. In other words, the Iranian migration involves a process of becoming immigrant in the receiving society. This implies that the Iranians generally have not arrived in this country with the intention of becoming permanent residents. It is through the period of studentship or internship that he learns to become immigrant. The data show that only 20 percent arrived here as intentional permanent immigrants. It must be added that 10 percent of those with immigrant visas constitute the Iranian minority groups of Jews, Armenians, and Bahai's. These Iranian ethnic and religious groups have a different pattern of migration, and usually come to the United States with a firm intention to remain.

Second, the Iranian migration is essentially the migration of middle class, highly trained professionals. It also contains a selective contingent of American-trained Persian professionals. As members of middle class Iranian families, the immigrants even before their arrival have to a great extent been predisposed to American culture. Thus, in terms of familiarity with America, unlike the early immigrants, they have no hard time to find their way in the new environment. However, it is mainly through educational and training experience in this country that the immigrants become motivated toward settlement.

The process of becoming an immigrant involves the changing of status from student or trainee to permanent immigrant. Thus, by the time the individual decides to over-stay, he is already well acclimated to American society. In fact, educational institutions, serving as social anchorages, have familiarized him with the American scene and have bridged his status with the larger society. The larger society, which has a great need for highly trained professionals, welcomes him into the professional structure and permits him to operate competitively within its relatively open market.[8]

Therefore, it is partly due to the immigrant's status and partly to contemporary post-industrial American society that the immigrant can see the realization of his professional and economic goals without the assistance of his countrymen. This condition has made it possible for the whole group to live as a group of scattered individuals with no real need for a collectivity or locality of its own.

The Immigrant without Community[9]

Community means the lasting relationship among individuals which could be characterized by a high degree of personal intimacy and social cohesion. It is frequently assumed that, when a number of immigrants together face an alien and hostile environment, a strong cohesive group, a community life, will develop. Such assumptions are usually based upon the initial experience of settlers confronted with discriminatory treatment by a dominant group. The very status of their minority situation has demanded the establishment of community life and a *Gemeinschaft* relationship. But when we find a group of professionals who represent a new type of mobile immigrant, it is evident that we can expect the immigrants to display a different pattern of in-group relations.

In his attempt to search for the Iranian community, the author has discovered that the immigrants who are the subject of this study are physically and socially isolated individuals. In other words, the Iranian immigrant's community, strictly speaking, has not developed. By Iranian community we mean a social process of interaction in which interpersonal ties are sustained and constantly renewed through frequent face-to-face interactions. As a form of processing community, the Iranian immigrants in America display an inadequate institutional structure. They are a community of a special type. They are a community if by community we mean a group of self-conscious people with a strong we-feeling who follow a way of life and a common pattern of "habit of thought" which mark them out as different from other ethnics in this country. But it is not a community in which the existing we-feeling has led to a dependency feeling or to mutual obligations among its members. Thus what is found is a community in process characterized so far by the lack of institutional completeness and social cohesiveness. The Iranian community constitutes a group culture in which there is hardly enough consensus and cooperation for it to be called a community. Its members basically live as individuals or as a series of separate and isolated families who do not come together as a national community except at *Now-ruz*—the Persian New Year-festivities annually. Otherwise, as an ethnic group the American Iranians live under conditions of total anonymity.

According to Judith Kramer, "the culturally distinctive institutions of the immigrants were necessary, if not sufficient, conditions of community in minority situations." She goes on further to say that "without such institutional resources, there is an absence of community, or at least an adequate community, with all the ensuing consequences of personal and social disorganization."[10] In the present study it was found that the Iranian community consists essentially of a network of interpersonal relations. Beyond this informal network, it has no organization with a capacity to attract or organize its members within its social boundaries.

Although there exist quite a few formal associations, such as Iran House (the political association of Iranian students) and the Iran Club (a nonpolitical association of Iranians in New York), none of them is considered the representative organization of the community. Almost a majority of the respondents did not affiliate or identify themselves with any of them. From the immigrants' point of view, the Iranian community is divided into two sub-communities: political and non-political. The political community represents the involuntary immigrants, most of whom are, paradoxically, students who are organized as a political group and because of their involvement in anti-government activities are not able or willing to return home. The non-political community is an abstract community in the sense that it has no organization of its own. Among the respondents in this study only a small percentage admitted that they have had affiliation or membership in the political community.

Since the idea of return is a dominating element with the majority of the immigrants, it is commonly believed that organizational affiliation of any sort has potentially negative effects upon their decision to return. Because the immigrant's present life is viewed as a temporary life, no attempt is made to establish any permanent affiliation. Even a professional organization of physicians does not exist (1977). When the Iranian physicians were asked why they did not have an organization similar to the Association of Turkish Physicians in the United States, 60 percent said it was because they had not yet decided whether to remain or return home. Another 40 percent believed that it was due to the extreme individualistic attitude of those who had no desire for any communal relationship.

The observations on the ethnic community in America indicate that the traditional ethnic community was built around the family and the church. In the case of the Iranians, neither of these institutions is transplanted or reconstructed in the new environment.[11]

With regard to the family, the Iranian migration is an individual migration. Thus, even for those who have established their own new family, the family in the Iranian sense is left behind at home. From the immigrant's point of view the extended family at home still remains the only source of primary relations. Although the immigrant is physically separated from his family at home, his psychological needs dictate that he be constantly in touch with the relatives at home. Seventy percent of the informants said that they had visited their family twice in the last few years. The majority of the individuals had invited one or two members of their family to this country. Almost 40 percent said that they made phone calls once a month to Iran. Thus it is a strong attachment to the family which makes Iranian immigrants, especially the undecided ones, view their new family as an integral part of the family at home.

Religious organization in the Iranian community is undeveloped, and the community exists without mosque or actual religious participation.

EXISTING INSTITUTIONS

Political Organization

The Iranian Students' Association in the United States (ISA), the oldest such organization, was founded in 1953. It emerged out of the Iranian Student Conference held on the campus of the University of Denver.

Originally the basic objectives of the Iranian Students' Association were:

1. To promote sincere cooperation among Iranian students in the United States
2. To protect rights of Iranian students without regard to their religious or political beliefs
3. To extend every possible help and guidance to Iranian students in the United States
4. To disseminate true information about Iranian people and their culture, history, problems, and aspirations
5. To present Iranian culture in the United States
6. To promote understanding with various student organizations in and outside the United States[12]

As these objectives indicate, the ISA was at first a-political, but since the early 1960s, with a drastic change in its political direction, it has become an outpost of the Iranian student movement. Although it was declared an illegal organization by the Iranian government, it remained up to 1977 the most vocal and active opposition to the Iranian regime.

The majority of the respondents, for obvious reasons, do not associate themselves with the ISA. In fact, some of the respondents are even critical of the ISA's leftist orientation. They believed that the ISA's extensive anti-government activities make it problematic for non-active Iranians to participate in cultural and social events. As a few individuals stated, "because everybody is afraid to be identified as a political activist." One even said:

> I changed my address in order not to receive the ISA's publications.

Another stated:

> The majority of the Iranian immigrants in the U.S. do not disclose their names, because they do not want their names on the students' mailing lists.

It should be noted, however, that in this sample there were a few individuals who, while no longer politically active, identified themselves with the aims of ISA.

The Immigrants' Press

There were at least three well-known newspapers which were published for the Iranian community in America.[13] Two of them were published weekly in Iran and were sent to subscribers by air. One was *Kayhan Airmail Edihon* and the other was *Etelaat Airmail Edition.* They were published by two of the major Iranian newspapers. The aims of these newspapers were to keep Iranians abroad—especially students and professionals—in touch with the progress of events at home and to help those abroad to return home. They contained general news, socio-economic affairs, art, and recently, a new section advertising jobs in Iran for those seeking desirable positions in the home country.

Since 1973, both papers have systematically published letters and articles encouraging return to Iran; often there have been written by former political activists or repatriated people. The editors believe that since most of the Iranians abroad are either misled or misinformed about the actual situation at home, such letters will help them to reconstruct a favorable image of the Iran of today. Although the articles have called for Iranians abroad to express their views on the difficulties of return, only a few readers have responded; the others, because of deep-rooted cynicism or other obvious reasons, have not replied.

A third newspaper—the only Persian language paper published in America—is *Iran Times.* Although it is designated as a "newspaper for the Persian speaking community in the United States and Canada," it is, in fact, a copy of the other two newspapers. Most of its contents include news and issues concerning home conditions. Its material concerning the condition of the Iranian community in America is limited and does not reflect actual problems or issues in the community.

In a sense, this paper and its orientation reflect the uncertainty which is inherent in the Iranian community. Unlike other immigrants' newspapers in the U.S. which aim to reinforce the establishment of national communities, the *Iran Times* seems to maintain a paradoxical dual position. On the one hand, it tries to bring together Iranians in their own community; on the other hand, it encourages them to return. The common belief held by Iranian newspapers is that Iranians, in general, have no acceptable reason to create a second Iran while the real Iran "opens its arms to receive them."

We must add that the *Iran Times,* with a large circulation, is the only Persian language paper and, thus, to some extent it has established a communication between various sections of the community. This is especially true in regard to businessmen, those in Iran and those in America who deal with Iranians at home and in America. Its advertisement section contains ads about Iranian restaurants, cultural institutes, travel agencies.

Moreover, through its one English language page, it has bridged the Iranian community and American society. The contents of this page include major political and economic matters, especially those of interest to the American business community, and cultural lessons for the American public. In terms of Persianization of Americans, especially those who are married to Iranians, this section renders a considerable service. It contains instruction ranging from the Persian language to the art of Persian cooking. This English language section of the *Iran Times* has even attracted the interest of major political figures of the United States. In 1973 and 1974, on the occasion of the Persian New Year, the Iran Times published a special edition in which greetings appeared from numerous cabinet members, senators, and congressmen.

Among the Iranians surveyed in this study the majority of informants were not subscribers to any of the three papers. Of 105 persons only 12 receive newspapers from Iran and 25 are regular readers of the Iran Times. The reasons cited for this lack of interest in newspapers included lack of time, indifference, and distrust of any Iranian newspapers.[14]

The Institution of Now-ruz

Now-ruz, the Persian New Year, coincides with the first day of spring, March 21—the vernal equinox. Now-ruz is the only time that Iranians in America come together as a national group.

The celebration of Now-ruz at parties is the most impressive expression of the Iranian cultural heritage and of national identification. Almost in every major city Now-ruz festivities are mounted for Iranians to celebrate. Usually committees are set up to sponsor the parties.

The existence of various New Year's parties also manifests the polarization of the Iranian community in America. There are generally two different kinds of Now-ruz parties in major cities. One is the so-called dolatiha (government sponsored) and the other is siyasiha (sponsored by the Iranian Student Association for political immigrants and students). Sometimes a third party is added under the name of bitarafha (neutrals). Therefore, Iranians are apt to attend these parties according to their affiliation with one or the other of the orientations. Of course, there are some individuals who attend both parties. As one such man said:

> I attend dolatiha's party because my wife loves formality. I also attend the students' party because they have a program which represents Iran and Iranians.

Another individual, who considers himself a neutral, said:

> I consider myself a non-political person, but still I prefer to go to the students' party because I feel more at home. Moreover, I can meet many of my former friends.

The Now-ruz party is the only major national event for the Iranian in America. As the only publicly visible ceremony, it creates an atmosphere of national identity and a sense of belonging. However, it seems that somehow the ceremony has lost the meaning originally attached to it. For example, one of the most important aspects of Now-ruz is to renew or to extend friendships. The Iranians who attend the festivities in America are apt to come together as strangers and to leave without exchanging addresses or gaining any new friendship. Most of the festivities are characterized by a lack of intimacy and excessive self-consciousness in maintaining a social distance. With respect to this point, one man said:

> I have attended New Years parties for five years. Each year I met different people at my table. Each time I tried to get their addresses—even their last names—but out of at least twenty people, only five were willing to exchange such information. Even those who give their phone numbers do not expect you to call them or pay a visit.

The Practice of dowreh

Dowreh consists of an informal group of contemporaries and familiars who meet on a regular basis, usually rotating the place of meeting among homes of members. My data show that the practice of dowreh among the informants was the exception, not the rule. Only 5 percent of the informants indicated that they had a sort of familial dowreh once a month. The reason for the lack of participation in such events was usually expressed in terms of the character of American urban life and Iranian orientation—i.e., individualism, distrust, and rigidity of social behavior.

CHAPTER 6

Communal Relationship and Structural Strains

For Max Weber, the communal relationship is based upon a sense of group solidarity resulting from the emotional or traditional attachments of the participants. "It is only when this feeling leads to mutual orientation of their behavior toward each other that communal relationships arise among them."[1] With regard to Iranian immigrants, the main point is that the communal relationship has not led to an in-group cohesiveness. In other words, the immigrants who are the subject of this study do not come together in significant and lasting relationships and are not interpersonally integrated individuals.

From the immigrant's point of view, the Iranian community consists of socially isolated individuals whose in-group relations lack frequency and duration. It is commonly believed by the informants that "Iranians in the United States live as individuals and in no way come into lasting contact with each other." One of the informants stated:

> I have a feeling of closeness with the Iranians who are close to me, but I would not say that it is a sense of community—because I know that it does not exist.

The data show that the immigrants display a high degree of independence in interpersonal relations with each other. Fifty-two percent of the respondents did not have social contacts of a regular nature with other Iranians. Twenty percent reported having absolutely no contact with other immigrants. Only 25 percent of the immigrants said that they had regular social contacts with each other. But even they added that such contacts did not involve mutual commitment and reciprocity. This is further expressed by the fact that 80 percent of the informants believed that the most undesirable feature of the Iranians in the United States was the lack of in-group relations and of involvement in face-to-face relationships.

Thus the majority of immigrants, in Alfred Schutz's term, view themselves and the fellow immigrants as contemporaries, not consociates. One frequently hears that "most of the Persians whom I meet are not my type" and "Iranians around me are not my type, they are just Iranians. I have nothing to do with them. We live an anonymous life."

The Iranian immigrants represent one of the most conscious groups, as a nationality, but, because of certain cultural and situational factors, this sense of nationality has not led to a mutual obligation toward social interaction. This confirms Max Weber's assertion that the ethnic community itself is not a community; it only facilitates types of "communal relationships."[2] The immigrants as a whole view themselves as a group rather than as a community. As a group they are disintegrated and isolated. They are mostly atomized individuals with few lasting relationships and show no tendency toward any common action. Although they place a high value upon sentimental relations and display community sentiment, the group as a whole does not possess a recognizable structure.

STRUCTURAL STRAINS

The concept of structural strains is a useful one in explaining the lack of the community-like life of the immigrants in this study. By structural strains I mean the destructive tendencies which are superimposed upon the immigrants' present situation. With regard to in-group relations, it was found that the respondents in general display an unusual lack of group cohesiveness. Contrary to the common prediction that the immigrants' anxiety leads to high community cohesiveness, Iranian immigrants, because of certain constraints, show little community spirit or even liking for one another.

Probably it is true that geographical dispersion and demographic conditions have cut off individuals from each other. But, as is noted by the students of community and ethnic groups, the lack of sufficient population density alone cannot fully explain the prevailing social isolation of an immigrant group. It is possible for the members of a community to be spatially separate but socially and culturally in contact.

This is especially true in the case of the immigrants' situation in the United States, where it is now possible to have interaction beyond the stage of local areas. In a recent observation Maurice Stein suggests that "a spatial neighborhood may have no significant meaning... True communal congeniality may exist between people scattered throughout a community." Stein stresses as the basis of the community a configuration of values and a set of institutional patterns, "a definite social identity, and primary group ties and primary relations..."[3] Thus, it is possible that cultural factors and situational aspects could always create barriers quite as effective as those of geographical factors in the prevention of a community formation.

In the case of the Iranian's self-isolation, the crucial question we must pose is what elements of strain have prevented cohesive in-group relations. In other words, why do the Iranian immigrants, despite a high degree of national consciousness and a definite cultural identity, tend to "escape from each other" or at least tend not to hold together? Even when demographic conditions seem to be suitable for such communal relationships, why is it that the forces for isolation are greater than the forces for cohesion and solidarity? To answer these questions, we must examine two sets of interconnected cultural and socio-political factors. Cultural factors imply the shared orientation of the immigrants which is brought here from the home society. Socio-political factors imply the socio-political condition of the immigrants in their present situation.

Perhaps the dominant theme of the immigrants' situation in America is its political character. The present community of Iranian professional immigrants in the United States is an outgrowth of the Iranian student population both in Iran and abroad. The Iranian student movement and its political organization since the early 1950s have had a great influence both directly and indirectly upon the attitudes of the present immigrants. In fact, for some of them the student movement has been a personal experience.

Because of the conspicuous absence of any other organization, the political association of students has dominated the entire Iranian community. Thus, as a result of political overtones, the entire structural relationship of Iranians in America tends to be infused with politics.

Since the in-group relations of the immigrants are influenced by such a political atmosphere, the majority of the immigrants—especially the neutrals—deliberately isolate themselves and take refuge outside the community. They stay away on the ground that association with Iranians will eventually lead to political discussions and position taking.

While the condition of mutual trust does not exist and the individuals' concerns are understood to be individualistic, community is difficult to achieve and even more difficult to retain. In this situation social participation seems pathological in itself. That is, from the immigrant's point of view any kind of affiliation or involvement is considered disruptive both for the group and for the participating individual. The result is that the majority of the immigrants who wish to have in-group relations remain outside their own ethnic community.

CULTURAL BAGGAGE OF THE IMMIGRANT

Professor Stanford M. Lyman writes that "the immigrant's cultural baggage needs sociological inspection to ascertain its effect on community organization."[4] Robert Nisbet also reminds us that "a knowledge of man's actual behavior in society must from the outset take into consideration the whole stock of norms and cultural incentives which are the product of social history."[5]

In the case of the Iranian immigrants it seems that most of the strains imposed upon their community are rooted in their cultural heritage. Because whatever is the logic of their social relations is in essence the logic of their culture, which here is reinforced by the socio-political factors of their present situation. Thus, in order to explain all forms of relationships, both formal and informal, between immigrants, we must discover those elements of the Iranian ethos which dominate the actual behavior of the immigrants.

Iranian Individualism

We pointed out earlier that of all the cultural traits among the Iranians the one most generally accepted and most influential has been individualism. In contrast to the majority of the immigrants who brought to America a tradition of communal life and a dependency feeling, the Iranian carried an extreme form of individualism. Therefore, even in his new environment, the Iranian continues to emphasize his own personal interest and avoid personal commitment to others.

It is quite clear that this form of individualism has a great impact upon interpersonal relations and the extent of communal life among the immigrants in this country. Especially when this trait is accompanied by the inherent uncertainty of the immigrants' status, one may expect to find a group characterized by a lack of sense of community. As the data reveal, there is an over-belief in the self-sufficiency and privacy of the respondents. Thus:

> I do not need to associate with other Iranians because everybody is concerned about his own personal interest.

> I have come to the conclusion that excessive contacts among us lead to manipulation and hostility.
>
> Here it is just like Iran, even two brothers find it safer not to get involved.
>
> We never become a group; the Iranian is born individualistic.

Such comments were expressed by a majority of the informants.

The fact that Iranians in America find it difficult to form a community or even a lasting social circle when they live close to one another is further confirmed by the following remarks of one of the respondents:

> I have lived in this neighborhood over seven years. Several times I have tried to organize other Iranians who live here into a social circle, but each time I face different problems. In most cases, after one meeting we found that the majority of the participants did not respect each other's opinions and showed no interest in maintaining family gatherings. Thus, several of us decided to form a sports team instead of a family dowreh. This time we failed, too. Our volleyball team, which was composed of ten physicians with a few other mature Iranians, did not last more than two weekends. Even in our game, nobody had respect for the others' rights. Everybody wanted to play in his own way. Our team ended up with a fight, and we had to give up the idea of togetherness.

The meaning of these over-emphasized beliefs in individualism and self-interest is clear. The result is that, as in Iran, the interpersonal relations of the immigrants operate in such a way that, actually, each person remains socially isolated and overtly self-concerned.

Iranian Insecurity, Cynicism, and Mistrust

There are other cultural traits which have serious consequences for the social life of Iranian immigrants. As noted in Chapter 2, these traits still dominate the mind of the individual Iranian. Having such cultural traits, being part of a generation of politically alienated Iranians, and living an uncertain life as undecided immigrants, these men and women exhibit such orientations in an extreme manner. A Persian saying often heard—"We do not know where we stand, we do not know whom we should trust"—indicates the extent of the prevailing insecurity and mistrust among the respondents.

Mistrust and insecurity are the dominant aspect of in-group relations among the respondents. This state of mind has produced in them a nihilistic outlook of cynicism and disenchantment in regard to any kind of communal relationship or social commitment. Consequently, one finds that almost 80 percent of the respondents strongly believe that "they simply do not trust each other." It is obvious that no community can be formed or sustained without at least some measure of mutual trust.

Moreover, having a belief that "no Iranian can be seriously trusted" has made the individuals extremely conscious of their present situation. Therefore, it is a normal mode of behavior for an Iranian "to escape from other Iranians,' or "to ignore him wherever he meets one," or even to "live in the same building or attend the same school without any interest in getting together."

This kind of attitude has also created a feeling of self-dislike among some of the Iranians. Although the informants pretended to like Iranian friendships and social gatherings, the majority of them believed that Iranians are too arrogant and unworthy of trust. It is obvious that in most cases such self-hatred is not a group self-hatred like that in some other minority groups.[6] Rather, it is a reaction against the feeling of insecurity and suspicion which the immigrants brought with them from the home society. As one informant said:

> We deliberately avoid in-group relations because in any group action, betrayal, or at least the fear of it, is commonplace.

In short, the group solidarity peculiar to any minority is not confirmed by the Iranian community. The community as a whole suffers from mutual distrust and lack of social commitment. The immigrants' state of mind is one of skepticism and distrust.

Situational Uncertainty

By situational uncertainty I mean the uncertainty surrounding the undecided immigrant, who lacks stable spatial and social anchorage. When an immigrant continues to remain undecided about his permanent place and maintains an attitude of some day returning, he is unable to establish any kind of lasting relationship. The following comments are representative of such attitude:

> We do not know what will happen the next day. We are postponing everything until we return to Iran.

One informant who has lived in America more than ten years said:

> Our home is Iran and our friends are there. Here we live a temporary life.

As noted above, although all the immigrants are officially permanent residents, the majority of them continue to remain belataklif (undecided) When asked for the date they plan to leave for Iran, few can give definite plans. Among the undecided immigrants the majority of individuals say they will return some day, ensha Allah (if God be willing). As one of the respondents said,

> Everyone I meet either is leaving or thinking of leaving.

Understandably, such an unstable situation—based as it is upon a precarious social climate—has clear implications for the individual's social life. The data reveal that this situation has seriously inhibited lasting intra-personal relationships and has discouraged any sort of general social involvement. Since the future is not clear—or, in the immigrants' words, "No one has seen tomorrow"—and the present environment is out of control, any social relationship is thought to have far-reaching effects upon the future. Thus, ironically, the immigrant who is committed to return finds out-group relations less problematic and far safer. As several respondents said,

> Iranians in this country prefer to live aloof because of political climate.

Another stated,

> In such a polarized community, the basic rule is that everyone must concern himself with his own immediate interest and nothing else.

But unwillingness to participate in in-group relations is not to be confused with lack of social competence.

IMMIGRANT TYPES AND IN-GROUP RELATIONS

As we have seen, the immigrants' responses to the common situation of "dual marginality" vary; that is, each type displays a different pattern of behavior and reaction from the others. This is also true with regard to immigrants' responses to the larger community in America. Therefore, the following discussion focuses on each type's in-group reaction.

The Ambivalent Iranian

This type generally shows an intensive desire toward social contact with other Iranians. His interest in such interaction stems from his cultural as well as psychological needs. This is especially true in the case of unmarried Iranian women and those married persons who constitute an Iranian couple. But precisely because of the temporary state of his life and his concern for return, the ambivalent Iranian is excessively sensitive toward associations with other Iranians. One of the immigrants reported:

> Our situation is unstable in this country. We love to meet other Iranians and to establish a sort of dowreh. But people are generally suspicious of one another.

Said another informant:

> We can have social gatherings only with those whom we know from home. If we meet an Iranian here, we do not know whom we are meeting. People try to hide their true personalities. Besides, our wives may not get along with each other.

In comparison with other types, the ambivalent Iranian still tends to have the most frequent social contacts with others. However, due to his specific social situation, he finds it "safer" not to extend his social contacts beyond relatives or friends whom he knew from Iran. That is, even if he lives in the same area with other Iranians, he is reluctant to establish lasting and reciprocal relations with those whom he does not know well.

The Persian Yankee

The orientation of the Persian Yankee toward the Iranian community can best be described as symbiotic rather than social. He has the least possible association with Iranians. If he has any, it is confined to his Iranian colleagues or his Iranian business partners. Because he is the most Americanized Iranian, he finds himself in conflict with those who still have not given up their hope of returning home. This is especially true in the case of those who have non-

Iranian wives. Since Iranian social gatherings are dominated and directed by Iranian men, and include Persian conversation, Iranian jokes, Iranian music, and Iranian food, the whole situation seems to be unpleasant for non-Iranian wives. As one husband said:

> We never met an Iranian for the second time because my former wife had no interest in such meetings. Some of us are so homesick that whenever we meet each other, we simply forget that our American wives are sitting next to us.

There is another problem for Iranians with non-Iranian wives which results from the lifestyle and the Americanized mode of behavior of these people. The Persian Yankee is a settled immigrant who has already internalized different forms of values concerning his social life. Thus he can no longer tolerate the Iranian formal code of social behavior. He likes to participate in social events for pleasure, rather than to impress others or claim prestige for his professional status. Since most Iranian parties turn out to be a marketplace for the display of individual lifestyles and social status, about which the members are extremely self-conscious, the Persian Yankee finds it difficult to take part in them. Such comments as the following are heard:

> I do not like to participate in Iranian parties because everybody wants to tell you how important he is.

> Persians are so sensitive to what you say and do.

> Everybody wants to be treated according to his title and position.

> People are rigid and self-conscious. It is difficult to exchange ideas and have conversation without being insulted.

> Iranians cannot tolerate opposite points of view. You cannot have a conversation for the sake of conversation with Iranians. They become emotionally involved.

As such comments indicate, the Persian Yankee either has no social relations with other Iranians, or, if he has any, they are mostly confined to those who have a similar status and way of life and, more importantly, have non-Iranian wives.

Self-Exile

This type of immigrant is an in-grouper Iranian. When he was an activist, he had a great involvement in the Iranian community. His actual behavior toward other Iranians was influenced by his political interest rather than by his social needs. Although today he is no longer an activist, he still maintains his affiliation with the political community. He regards his social contact with other Iranians as part of his "mission" and his national commitment. As one of the informants put it:

> My contact with other politically minded Iranians is today limited to phone calls. The only way to establish some sort of community is phoning. My family and professional responsibilities do not permit me to exchange visits with other Persians. But still I have a strong desire to get in touch with my former friends. In this way you do not feel isolated, at least.

Despite this national commitment the involuntary immigrant today is an isolated person. Withdrawal from political activities has resulted in social and physical isolation from most of his former friends. His social contact with non-political Iranians does not lead to lasting and reciprocal relations. Since the political immigrant has no reason to mask his political ideas and has a tendency to publicize himself as a victim, the non-political Iranians view him as a threat to the maintenance of their social gatherings.

There are indeed several instances where such an individual has participated in an Iranian party which soon disintegrated and the attendants at which avoided getting together with him again. Several informants pointed out that "if people find out that you have invited a well-known political Iranian, they soon identify you with that person and they no longer like to visit you."

The Committed Professional

This type of immigrant—like the Persian Yankee—has no real interest in establishing communal relationships with other Iranians. He is not bound as others are by ethnic or national conventions. He displays a stronger tendency to associate with members of his profession alone. His interest in seeking status within his professional group militates against his ethnic and sentimental relations. Therefore, his closest friends are usually other foreign professionals or professionals of the host society. Even if he finds himself among other Iranians, he tends to count himself more as a man of academia than as a Persian. Thus:

> It does not make any difference with whom I am associating, as long as he is not a prejudiced person.

Said another, expressing a strong sense of professional identity:

> I am no longer a Persian in a real sense. My interests lie in my professional community.

Still another informant viewed himself as a member of the international community, saying:

> I am a citizen of the world, and I can relate myself to everyone else.

The fact that this type of immigrant insists on being a "citizen of the world" while he is an Iranian results from his overreaction to his professional status. At the same time, by underestimating his national commitment he wants to release himself from any social responsibility toward his own people. This, of course, becomes a source of creativity and professional growth for him.

CHAPTER 7

The Immigrant and Out-Group Relations

With this overview of in-group relations we now turn to the character of out-group relations. The remarkable thing about Iranian immigrants is their rapid adaptability to American society and its basic values. As highly qualified immigrants, they have benefited from the very urban qualities that fitted them for participation in middle class American life. But as we pointed out earlier, the Iranians tend to live a marginal social life in the United States. Some 90 percent of our respondents report that their circle of close friends is composed exclusively of Iranians. Such self-isolation or marginality is explained by two important factors: the class background of the individual immigrant and the cultural consciousness of the Iranians as a group.

In his discussion of immigrants' marginality Stonequist writes: "The individual who has emigrated from the higher classes of a nationality with a proud and self-conscious history finds it especially difficult to identify himself with the new country."[1] Stonequist's argument has particular relevance to the Iranian. The Iranian immigrant is typically a middle class professional with a proud and self-conscious national identity. At the same time, he is uncertain, unintended immigrant and perceives his present situation as a temporary one.

Generally, the Iranian immigrant in the United States is not a stranger in his new environment. Through his period of studentship or internship, a period of information gathering, he has familiarized himself with the larger society. That is, he has become an immigrant in this country, involved in a network of interpersonal relations through which he has taken root in the larger society consciously or unconsciously.

INTERPERSONAL RELATIONSHIPS

With regard to interpersonal relationships, the main question is not why or how the host society accepts or rejects the immigrant, but to what extent the Iranian immigrant himself has accepted, or refused to be politically and socially integrated into, American society. We must remember that the immigrant is professionally and economically well accommodated in the larger society; his public life or professional life is characterized by an involvement in various activities. On the other hand, as a culturally conscious and middle class immigrant he has a private life of his own, dominated by his own cultural systems. Thus, in explaining the immigrant's interpersonal relations with the host members, it is his social life which calls for examination.

Under the assumption that the immigrant's relationship to American gatherings and social occasions may tell something about his relationship to broader units of social life, we asked the immigrant the following questions:

> How often do you visit in the homes of your American colleagues or neighbors,—never,—once a week,—once a month?
>
> How often do you invite your American neighbors or colleagues into your home,—never,—once a week,—once a month?

The data revealed an unusual degree of self-segregation among the respondents. Eighty percent of the respondents were socially isolated with no declared social contacts of a regular nature outside their own family. Only five percent of the sample members said they had regular social gatherings with their American colleagues. Another fifteen percent of the respondents who were married to Americans said they had occasional social gatherings with their relatives and friends.

This social isolation and the lack of intimate relationships are most striking when we realize that the immigrants, unlike low status immigrants, enjoy a greater opportunity for social contact with Americans. As a group of professionals they have regular face-to-face contacts with out-group individuals. However, most of these relations are based on secondary contacts—contacts in which the immigrants and the host members are related by a single role relationship; i.e., doctor-nurse or doctor-patient.

Another way to examine how well the immigrant is engaged outside of his group and how intensive that relationship is, has to do with the number of his intimate friends. Thus the question dealing with friendship was introduced as an indicator of some measure of intimate relationships. In response to the question "Have you made any intimate American friends since you have come to America?" the majority of the respondents said they had one or two, but they quickly added that "we have friends, but not in the Iranian sense of the word."

When the respondents were asked why they found it difficult to know an American whom they could consider as a close friend, the answers referred predominantly to the cultural differences of two nations. For example, several respondents who had Iranian wives explained the manifestation of cultural differences in the following way:

> To exchange friendships and invitations with Americans, I have to maintain double standards—American and Iranian. Thus I tend to reject invitations in order to prevent the conflict.

Among the respondents who had American wives there was a strong desire for interaction with Americans, but even this group displayed a sharp consciousness of the conflicting value systems of the two cultures. In fact, these individuals had achieved marital assimilation and were "structurally assimilated" yet were more critical of the American moral standard than other Iranians.

INTERMARRIAGE

Intermarriage of Iranians with non-Iranians, especially non-Muslims, is a new phenomenon. Just like Western education, it is a by-product of Iranian Westernization, and it was initiated by the first generation of Western-educated Iranians. While at home marriage even with a non-Muslim Iranian was and still is taboo, for an Iranian abroad it became fashionable to marry a Western woman and bring her home, despite his parents' disapproval.

The receptivity of Iranians abroad toward intermarriage can be explained in terms of their emancipation from parental control as well as a tendency toward assimilation of Western values and institutions. Being away from primary groups, having been resocialized by Western institutions, and most importantly, facing the problem of loneliness, the Iranian abroad looks with approval upon intermarriage.

As mentioned earlier, the frequency of intermarriage with Americans among members of this sample was very high. Out of 105 respondents, 39 persons were married to non-Iranians. Of the 39 intermarriages, 36 couples consisted of an Iranian man and an American wife.

Intermarriages of Iranians in this country have also a legal dimension. That is, marriage to an American citizen, for Iranians, is desirable in order to change a non-immigrant visa to a permanent immigrant visa. It is interesting to note that although such marriages are functional for readjustment of the individuals in this country, in most cases they become dysfunctional with regard to the individuals' decision to return home. The intermarried individuals defend their marriages despite the fact that their parents at home tend to disapprove of the alien bride (arous farangi). The common wish among Iranian families is to see sons and daughters not lost to a society culturally and religiously different from their own. Since such marriages militate against the return of their children, parents are especially anxious to discourage them. They often make their disapproval felt through letters reporting how many of these marriages have ended in divorce or have resulted in family disintegration.[1]

It must be noted, however, that in most cases, intermarriage has not necessarily led to extensive social contact with Americans. Not quite 10 percent of intermarried informants visit American in-laws and receive them at home. There are some indications that the oversensitivity of the Iranian toward his status as well as his cultural consciousness make it difficult for him to establish intimate contacts with his American in-laws. In such cases the wife is considered an "exceptional" member of American society, while her parents and relatives represent typical Americans. With regard to this point, several informants expressed their feelings in the following words:

> We usually have no social contact with Americans. My American in-laws live in our area, but we do not visit each other very often.

And another person, who sensed a loss of national status, said:

> I personally have no relation with my in-laws but because I cannot get along with them. They are very uninformed about Iranian people and their culture.

Still another, discussing his political ideas, stated:

> I avoid social contact with my in-laws because whenever we meet, I feel insulted over their image about my country.

Emphasizing the Iranian consciousness of national identity, this person believed:

> We Iranians are very self-conscious about our status and national identity. When we meet Americans, even if they are our inlaws, we somehow become defensive about our people and our values.

Another politically-minded Iranian said:

> I always criticize the American government's foreign policy and my in-laws feel very insulted. That is why we have decided not to get much involved with them.

Thus, even marital assimilation has not been effective in extending social involvement of Iranian immigrant individuals within the larger American society. In fact, intermarriage has somehow resulted in greater appreciation of the individual's cultural identity.

ASSOCIATIONAL PARTICIPATION

By associational participation of the respondents we mean the social and professional involvement of the individuals in public life as professionals. This aspect of the immigrants involvement was examined in the following questions:

> Are you a participant member of any local American club or association,—none,—one,—two or more? If you are a member of any professional organization, do you see yourself as an active member?—yes,—no.

Ninety percent of the respondents said they had no membership in any social club or association. Ten percent reported they had membership in one social club, mainly because of the interests of their American-born children. As a group of professionals, whose life is centered around their profession, they might be expected to enjoy a high degree of participation in professional organizations. But, while the majority of the physicians were members of the American Medical Association, only 15 percent of these viewed themselves as active members. A good deal of evidence suggests that the majority of the respondents tended to remain marginal, even in their professional and academic world. With regard to the extent of professional involvement, such as writing books and publishing articles, the Iranian Ph.Ds had a greater involvement than the physicians.

IMMIGRANT TYPES AND OUT-GROUP RELATIONS

Also, in terms of response to American society, Iranian immigrants are not a homogeneous group. Because of differing patterns of expectation, each type of immigrant grouping relates in a different way to America.

Ambivalent Iranian

Not unexpectedly, of the four types of immigrants, the ambivalent Iranian tends to have the least social contact with Americans. Moreover, he has also the most unfavorable attitude toward American society.

In terms of discontent with American society, the ambivalent Iranian differs sharply from the other three types, because the home community tends to remain the only source of his primary relations. In a sense, he is a home-going person whose future life is oriented toward the home society. To him life in America is a sort of temporary halt on the way to the homeland. Much of his unfavorable attitude toward America is caused by a basic uncertainty inherent in his present status as an undecided immigrant. As one often hears, "I am not interested in American values because I am not an immigrant. I must remain Iranian in case I go home."

Thus, with regard to structural assimilation, the ambivalent Iranian usually lacks any initial inclination to assimilate. This is not to say that he is not subjected to a process of unconscious assimilation. However, his feeling of temporariness creates an extremely unfavorable attitude toward Americanization. As one informant, who continued to remain an undecided person for ten years, stated:

> I still cannot reconcile myself to the idea of becoming a naturalized citizen and staying here all my life.

Another who has become a citizen of the United States said:

> Although I received my citizenship papers here ten years ago, I never cast my ballot, or did write any letter to the elected politicians in my town. I have basically remained an Iranian.

It is due to such undecidedness that he has not yet been able to free himself from his cultural ties and his attachment to his homeland. He still expects to return to Iran, of which he thinks he has intimate knowledge and in which he has long-waiting "welcomers." Thus he remains in a constant emotional and cultural conflict with the host society, and tends to blame it for some of his frustrating experiences.

In short, the out-group relations of the ambivalent Iranian are fraught with ambiguity and conflict. Fifty years ago, when there were perhaps quite few Persians in America, Robert E. Park classified Iranians, among other minor nationalities, "as exotics, because for various reasons they are, or seem to be, more completely isolated and removed from contacts and participation in American life than any other immigrant people."[2] The particular reason for this is unknown to us, for there is a lack of evidence. What is striking is that the ambivalent Iranian, who is an American trained professional, is indeed removed from contact and participation with Americans and lives an isolated life in the larger society.

Persian Yankee

This type of immigrant is usually interested in a long-run adjustment to his present environment. He displays a proclivity toward social relations with his American colleagues. Marital assimilation and professional involvement compel him to enter into contact with Americans. Thus he is open to accept changes in his present position.

With regard to assimilation, he not only views it—up to a certain point—as a positive value, but he has also accepted it as an inevitable process. He is well aware that if he wants to be a successful professional in America he needs to have an intimate knowledge of American values and standards.

It is for this type of immigrant that migration has resulted in a release from patriotic obligation and family attachments. In fact, as a result of his acquaintance with new norms and values, he has found a basis for comparison between the host society and his own homeland. The outcome of such unfounded comparisons is a deep dissatisfaction with his own society and a great enthusiasm for the host society. As a first generation immigrant he might experience some sort of cultural alienation, but he tends to accept that as a price for his acculturation.

Committed Professional

This type of immigrant, also a settler, resembles the Persian Yankee. Similar to the Persian Yankee, he is a well-accommodated immigrant who has already internalized some of the basic values of the American society. The only difference between him and the Persian Yankee is that he is more committed to his profession; thus he is able to resolve his marginality by his commitment to his profession. Moreover, with regard to assimilation, he views himself as being "universalized" rather than Americanized. That is, he has developed a mode of living which is totally characteristic of neither society, his native society nor American society.

Self-Exile

This type of immigrant holds the most critical view toward the American political system. To this individual the American political system is imperialistic and conspiratorial. While he condemns the political system of his own country, he also has no respect for American political institutions. Ironically, he is a "guest" who has chosen his "enemy" as his host. However, it must be noted that the anti-American sentiments of this type of immigrant are not generalized against all Americans. According to him, it is the American capitalists, not the American people, who are his enemy. Therefore, he is not a "stranger" in Simmel's sense, with detachment and objectivity, but he is an insider whose response to his new environment is colored by rhetoric and ideological statements.

In response to the question "How much do you like America, personally?" the majority of this group indicated a great dislike of the host society. Attitudes of the respondents toward the Americans ranged from apathy to outright hostility. The majority of the respondents made the familiar charges, by no means limited to Iranians, that America's accomplishments have been technological and lacking in culture.

In Iranian gatherings and conversations the temptation to make some anti-American remarks is difficult to resist. It is a normal mode of behavior to despise and condemn the host community. Surprisingly, even those who had married Americans made no attempt to conceal their hostility toward American society. For example:

> The more I live here the more I think the Iranian culture offers a deeper meaning to human existence than American culture. I think Iranians must hold to their culture. It is a disgrace for an Iranian to become Americanized.

> I have no love for the American system because it is responsible for most of the misery of my people.
>
> Whenever I see the commercials of oil companies on the television, it reminds me of what American capitalism has done.
>
> No matter what you do here, you are still an alien and subject to various discriminations.
>
> I no longer believe in the American ideals because I have seen how these ideals are in reality overlooked.

Despite his hostility toward the American system, the involuntary immigrant is socially well adjusted to his present situation. He usually has extensive contacts with Americans, but only with those Americans of a radical and political type. He may even have social contacts with the members of various radical organizations of Third World people in this country.

The hostile response of this type of immigrant is not a result of unpleasant experiences in this country, for as a white professional man he is not subject to significant institutional barriers. His hostility is transferred from his home society and is intensified by his further radicalization in his present environment. Thus he looks upon his host society from an ideological perspective and finds it hostile and antagonistic.

As the immigrants' comments indicate, Iranian hostility toward America, in addition to the ideological dimension, as discussed in chapter 3, may be attributed to the immigrant's cultural consciousness as well as his immigrant status. In terms of cultural conflict, Iranians regard themselves as a community culturally superior to America. The immigrant, as an Iranian intellectual, is fully aware of the cultural identity and international standing of his country.

Moreover, the colonialized mentality as found among some of the immigrants does not exist among a majority of Iranian immigrants. Rather, the average Iranian immigrant views America as "a new state" which came into existence when Persian civilization was already flourishing. It is due to such cultural awareness that the immigrant might even be highly acculturated without being concerned about his ethnic identity.[3]

CHAPTER 8

The Immigrant and the Home Society

For us all other lands are disappointing.
—Iranian immigrant in America, 1972

The predominant orientation of the majority of the immigrants toward the home society is the expectation of eventual return. However, here again we cannot speak of immigrants as an undifferentiated group. Each type, according to its actual status, displays a different orientation toward home.

AMBIVALENT IRANIAN

This type of immigrant displays intense nostalgia toward the home society. The nostalgic feeling is central to the immigrant's mind. The majority of the respondents in this category strongly believed that they were missing something important. When they were asked what aspects of Iranian life was missed most, 90 percent stressed the absence of family and relatives. This was especially true of those individuals who were the only members of the family in this country. One informant said he knew of at least ten instances where the attachment to the family forced well-established physicians to return home after ten years of living here. Another person who has lived here for more than fifteen years—and already has bought a cemetery plot for the family—said he is thinking of returning because of his unsatisfied need to be among his own people.*

*Although no accurate official estimates are available with regard to reimmigration of the undecided Iranians after the 1979 Revolution, the author knows a relatively sizeable number of these Iranians who are now in Iran.

The nostalgic reaction for some is frequently accompanied by a sense of guilt, disguised or unrecognized, at having left home and having disappointed the welcomers. When it comes to such feelings, the immigrants usually talk of collective guilt and not individual guilt. For example:

> Iranians should not forget the home. They are more needed at home than here. Most of the Iranians have a sense of guilt that they are not returning home.

This type of immigrant also has a strong feeling of loss of personal status in his American environment. The significant difference between expected status at home and his present status makes him aware of a status inconsistency. The following typical comments were expressed by those who became disenchanted because of a loss of status:

> We Iranians in this country have succeeded economically and professionally, but socially we are dissatisfied. Here no one knows what we have achieved; even if they do, they do not care.

> My success in this country has not resulted in greater social recognition. I always have to introduce myself. But at home the people around me know who I am and what I have achieved. This gives me the feeling that I mean something more to them than to the people around me here.

> I have attained influence and prosperity, yet in terms of status and recognition, I feel that I am lost and unknown.

Thus it is in relation to his status community at home that the immigrant compares and contrasts his present status. He sees himself between two different status audiences. Each audience, offering its own standard of evaluation, provides him with a different status and gives him a unique recognition. Thus, as a result of this double standard of prestige ranking, the immigrant finds his status in America not comparable at any level to his status in Iran. When the individuals in this category were asked, "How do you compare your social standing in Iran with that in the United States,—higher in Iran,—higher in the US.,—the same?" the majority of the respondents admitted they have experienced severe loss of status.

If any status affinity exists among ambivalent Iranians, it is a feeling of not being able to enjoy the fruits of their success. This obviously causes a certain feeling of inadequacy. As one informant stated, "Those with whom I should share my success are not around me. This makes me only half-way successful."

Such an expressed feeling of status deprivation is understandable when it is recalled that in Iran such an individual enjoys relatively high prestige and a much wider public recognition. In fact, his personal success becomes his family's success; his social standing brings prestige also to his family—and even to his neighborhood. Furthermore, in all spheres of social activities, as a repatriated professional he is accorded a positive particular identity; he is the American-trained physician, the American-educated professor, or the American-trained nurse.[1] Here in America not only is his social recognition limited to areas such as hospitals and universities, but as an alien he is subject to a discriminatory treatment because of his particular identity; he is an alien physician, an alien professor, an alien nurse. It is as a result of such lowering of status that this type of immigrant finds that his professional success has not satisfied his social needs. Thus he remains—up to a certain point—an undecided immigrant, and he formulates plans for returning home.

The ambivalent Iranian displays a pervasive desire to return to his homeland. The tendency toward re-emigration is one of the main characteristics of this type of immigrant. While some of the advantages of the present environment may exert pressure upon him to remain in America, personal ties, status aspiration, and cultural attachment constantly evoke the hope of returning home. The image of "home," of course, is an over-idealized image. From a distance of time and space life at home is romanticized; this intensifies the tendency to return home. At the same time, the idea of returning gives the immigrant a convenient assurance against the temptation not to return home. Therefore, he constantly seeks information concerning his prospective position, at home and he tries to maintain a dialogue with those who have already established themselves at home.

With regard to the immigrant's uncertainty about returning home, the immigrants were asked to state why they had remained undecided concerning return to Iran. The reasons offered were an uncertainty about achieving professional advancement without having connections, jealousy on the part of the older generation of established repatriated professionals, and uncertainty about being able to readjust to the present situation in Iranian society.

PERSIAN YANKEE

This type of immigrant, who was for a while an undecided immigrant and even might have returned home to stay there, is today an Iranian-American and is no longer oriented toward returning home. He might advise other Iranians to return home, but he thinks that he himself has no choice. As one of the informants stated: "Those of us who have been here for more than ten years are no longer capable of changing our life. We have already established ourselves here. It is true we wish we could have returned home, but if we do so now, it is an injustice to our families, especially to our children."

His nostalgia toward the home society is no longer accompanied by a guilt feeling. This man believes he did his best to return home and stay there, but home failed to accept him as he was. Consequently, Iran forced him to return to this country, he feels. The home situation must be blamed. Such feelings are expressed in the following comments:

> I returned home to prove to my family that I prefer to live in Iran, but I realized that I no longer belonged there.

> I personally do not feel guilty about becoming an immigrant. I decided to become an American immigrant after I went home and stayed there for two years.

> When I married an American girl, I told her that I must return home and live there. But when we went back, we could not readjust ourselves to that situation.

Therefore, the fact that he tried to stay home but found it impossible to do so gives him some sort of satisfaction about his present situation. Even if he agrees that his action in coming back to this country was irresponsible, he denies full responsibility for it. That is, he has an excuse for not being able to fulfill his original goal.[2]

Since the Persian Yankee as a first generation immigrant has still some sort of nostalgic feeling toward his family and his homeland, he employs certain techniques to counteract them. For instance, he may pay a visit to Iran at least every other year. Those who have Iranian wives send their wives to Iran almost every summer. Some of the informants have invited their parents to come here and stay with them for a time. The most common technique among Iranian couples is making long distance telephone calls to their families at least two or three times a year. One of the informants in this category said, "Whenever I feel homesick I spend some of my vacation in Mexico. In this way I remind myself how difficult it is to live in an underdeveloped country."

Because he already has found a new reference group in this country, the Persian Yankee is less subject to status inconsistency than the ambivalent Iranian. He no longer compares his status with his former reference group at home. That is, as a result of his Americanization, he tends to accept the American standard of evaluation and feels satisfied with his present status. Even if as an alien professional he faces some status inconsistency, he tends to view it as the price for avoiding his maladjustment in an uncertain world at home. Thus he has reached the conclusion that he will be better off here than at home, for at home he would have compromised certain principles which to him are requisites for higher status.

Among the Persian Yankees there are a few woman professionals, Ph.D.s and physicians, who are facing what Everett Hughes has termed the "dilemma of status."[3] But should these individuals return home, they experience the same problem to a greater extent. That is, the marginality of these individuals is intensified at home, where engineer, scientist, and physician are traditionally expected to be male. Thus the status holder in these positions will have a greater difficulty in establishing integrity across roles and situations.

Despite the fact that the majority of the Persian Yankees have come to accept their present status, their Iranian wives are not fully satisfied with their present situation. The loss of status for these wives is manifested in an inability to exhibit material gains and be accorded high status. For example:

> At home I am a Khanum Doctor (doctor's wife), while in this country I am just a housewife.
>
> At home we feel more important and more comfortable. We will have a maid who will take care of everything.

Another technique in resolving this problem is to transfer the Persian institution of servant-master relationship to this country. There were several instances in which the Iranian couples asked their families at home to send them a maid (kolfat). In this way the wife could enjoy some of the prestige that she is missing in her present situation.

While the Persian Yankee does not suffer terribly from loss of status, there are indications that as an Iranian he does experience that loss. The immigrant's consciousness of his long-standing cultural heritage makes him think of himself as part of a national group vis-a-vis Americans. This awareness is accompanied by the feeling of national exclusiveness which permits him to view himself as deserving the respect and recognition of others. When he finds himself in a situation in which the people he meets have no particular recognition of his nation or have fallacious images of it, he feels a loss of national status. The majority of the informants in this category complained that Americans have no substantial knowledge of Iran. As one individual said, "I constantly must remind the Americans about Persian civilization and Iranian standing in the world."

With regard to Persian uniqueness, it is believed by the majority of the informants that the Iranian is a gifted person. "We Iranians have a special quality ."

As for other immigrant groups, such feelings of national exclusiveness have made the Iranian immigrant extremely sensitive to his status." I do not let people look at me as an ordinary immigrant." Such sensitivity sometimes involves overreaction and aggression. One of the immigrants said:

> I am the only person among the foreign physicians who objects to being treated as an alien. After one month of working in the hospital, I had fought with almost everyone.

Another informant stated:

> My supervisor does not know how to handle me because I always argue with her. I just cannot accept what she says, she has to convince me. I have to be like that because people might take advantage of me as a foreigner. I always tell my colleagues that Iranians cannot be manipulated.

This individual's notion of uniqueness is partly a reflection of Persia's achievement in the past, and it is partly due to the individual's achievements in relation to others in this country.

SELF-EXILE

This type of immigrant is more oriented toward return than are other groups. As an Iranian intellectual he feels a responsibility to return home and contribute to the well-being of his people. But since he is aware of his difficulty at home, he has no choice but to wait and see. He justifies his migration in terms of his "legitimate" political convictions.

In terms of the general condition of political immigrants, two distinctive orientations are emerging. One is an orientation of disillusionment with Iran which will lead to his becoming a permanent immigrant. In such cases, the individuals with such an orientation tend to become settlers and to give up the hope of returning home. Another orientation is toward depolitication and re-emigration. Passage of time and, more importantly, the changing situation at home are responsible for these two trends. Here are a few representative comments on these two ongoing trends.

> The political Iranians today constitute a community of passive resistance. At the present time, it is escape, perhaps more than anything else, which provides a motive behind their staying in this country. They have lost touch with the Iranian realities at home.

> Some of the political Iranians in this country continue to display a genuine idealism which is unrelated to harsh reality. Some of us who came to this country in our early twenties never had a chance to understand our own position in relation to the Iranian situation. We exiled ourselves without realizing that our goal was to finish our education and return home.

> I personally know a few former political activists who have come to the conclusion that they cannot do anything by remaining in this country. Some of these individuals are already engaged in their professional activities and because they have married Americans are no longer interested in returning. There are some others who are thinking of returning.

The following comments are representative of those whose orientations are leading toward compromise and return.

> After all these years of living and raising four children in this country, I no longer can tolerate self-exile. I am sure if I go home I will be more satisfied.

An engineer who is preparing himself to return and work from the inside of the "system" states:

> At the present time, the Iranian government invites the Iranian abroad to return home and accept responsibility in devel-

> oping the Iranian society. I personally do not think we have any other choice. I do see a chance to go home and work from the inside.

An Iranian who has had extensive political activities in this country and never thought he could return home says:

> I have come to the conclusion that I must return home and put an end to my fifteen year life of uncertainty. I even bought cemetery plots for my family and other Iranians. But right now I am negotiating with the Iranian officials in order to clear up my case and return home.

Another politically committed Iranian who has had a life which was political in the most decisive sense, stated his disillusionment:

> I came to this country fifteen years ago. I became a political activist and engaged in the student movement. My marriage was also a political marriage. She was an American girl and shared my political perspective. I must admit that our marriage failed because we underestimated our cultural differences and overestimated our political consensus. Politically, I am also a failure because my radicalization was not in tune with realities at home. I am planning to return home and do my best to adjust to the Iranian situation.

COSMOPOLITAN IRANIAN

This type of immigrant has usually no particular interest in re-emigration. To him it does not make any difference where he lives as long as he is able to achieve professional advancement. He resembles those scholars who consider themselves too educated for the Iranian environment, and thus tends to justify his migration in terms of the practical necessities of his profession.

This type of immigrant argues that as long as his country is unable to use his knowledge and training, it is to the interest of his profession to stay abroad and advance his knowledge. Thus he identifies himself more with the intellectual and scientific world than with his home society. Although he might have some other personal and political reason for Staying here, he usually overemphasizes his professional reason. Several of the informants in this category expressed their feelings in the following words. A scientist emphasizing his role as an international scientist said:

> I personally believe that if I stay here I will be able to contribute more to the prestige of my country than if I return home.

And another, putting a condition on his return, stated:

> I will return home when I find out that I can utilize my knowledge and training as I am doing here.

Still another noted in a similar vein:

> I feel committed to my professional standards; therefore I need an environment that can be conducive to my scientific activities. I am sure wherever I am I can contribute to the prestige of my people.

As these comments indicate, this type of immigrant tends to show his national commitment through maintaining an international outlook. That is, he believes that if he achieves international recognition as a scientist, his country will benefit. Therefore, in his present situation he seeks status within his professional group and gains professional satisfaction outside of his country. Iran for him constitutes a status threat—a situation which is thought to block his professional motivations. As far as his adjustment in this country is concerned, his cosmopolitan outlook as well as his identification with a new collectivity makes him less subject to continuous anxiety despite moments of strain.

CHAPTER 9

Immigrants and Their Children

Second Generation: Today's American

Children born in America to Iranian or Iranian American parents, or those who are brought to America young enough to receive their early socialization here, may be considered second-generation Iranian immigrants. As discussed earlier, the majority of Iranian immigrants arrived in the United States in the last twenty-five years. Most members of the second generation are today of school age and some just have begun to reach adolescence.[1]

Generally speaking, second-generation Iranians are born into families in which the level of material wealth, the area of residence, and the pattern of consumption are the same as that of professional Americans. The Iranian family in the United States, unlike the traditional family in Iran, usually consists of a man, his wife, and their two or three children. Emigration as an individual family's migration has separated the couple from all others who have lived with them in Iran. The Iranian family is also decidedly child-centered, and its patriarchial and authoritarian character is already undermined in the new environment. There is some evidence that among Iranian couples the institutionalization of equalitarian norms has already taken place, particularly in the area of child rearing.

The most pressing concern of all the parents is to provide the best quality of education for their children; in fact, the parents are obsessively concerned with the progress and educational achievement of the children. Personal achievement, curiosity, respect for authority, and, most importantly, following the father's profession are highly valued. For example, the son or daughter of an Iranian physician is encouraged to become a doctor. But the right of the child is recognized, and the child is encouraged to develop a sense of individuality. With regard to sex role socialization, the dominating view is still restrictive for girls. The unequal treatment of the two sexes is more prevalent among the Iranian couples.

In the traditional Iranian family, discipline was the indispensable instrument of child rearing. Strong emphasis was placed on the value of conforming to the patterns laid down by elders and avoiding any behavior that might bring discredit to the family.[2] The Iranian parents in this study stated that they do not approve of physical punishment and instead would discipline by reward and praise. In fact, permissiveness was observed in several cases. For instance, the parent lets the child know that the pace he or she is setting is acceptable. An Iranian wife pointed out that "my husband has finally become accustomed to requesting, not ordering." However, a child's aggression toward the parent, particularly among the Iranian couples, is not tolerated.

General and impressionistic observations of parent-child relationships suggest that there is a high expectation on the part of the parents, especially the fathers. "We are the best and brightest educated Iranians; we expect that our children follow our steps," was stated by several physicians.

The Iranian mother is the child's most important socializer, and it is from her that the child receives affection and in most cases unconditional love. The Iranian mother pays unlimited attention to the child, particularly a boy. In the absence of older people at home, such as grandmothers, the Iranian mother depends heavily on Dr. Spock and other experts for guidance. One hears frequent references to them.

In sum, unlike the second generation of other immigrants, the second generation Iranians receive an early socialization which involves a great amount of social-psychological absorption of the most subtle American middle class values, training, and behavioral patterns. The level of income they provide, the professional status they confer, and their assimilating tendencies allow the Iranian immigrants to provide their children with middle class way of life.

LANGUAGE AND IDENTITY

Most Iranian parents are bilingual; some even speak other languages such as French and German; but their children speak only English. According to the survey, the majority of children of Iranian couples and almost all children of mixed parenthood are unable to speak Farsi, except for some occasional Farsi words or terms of affection. None of the children can write in Farsi; sometimes the firstborn understands a little Farsi, but even those answer their parents in English when they speak to them in Farsi. It seems that the phenomenon of language loyalty found in some other immigrant groups has not prevailed among Iranian immigrant children.

The teaching of Farsi has not been a major concern of most Iranian parents. A few concerned parents have tried to teach Farsi at home or to organize Farsi classes on weekends; but none of these attempts has proved successful because "the children showed resistance" or "it interfered with other family affairs." The Iranian parents have failed to create a cultural atmosphere and orient their children to their own ethnic identity, especially the learning of the language. This resulted from:

1. Their small numbers in their residential area
2. Lack of physical proximity and social interaction with a large number of other Iranians
3. Lack of cultural and religious centers
4. Lack of firm commitment on the part of most parents to be bearers of their culture

As a result of all these factors, a large proportion of the children's social participation is taking place among Americans of their age and classes. Separated from other Iranian children and living in a cultural milieu which contains no significant element of their own cultural heritage, the Iranian child experiences a childhood which is extensively American. Although they belong to a culturally distinctive family, the children do not display consciousness of their distinctiveness as a group. At the neighborhood or at school the Iranian child has no distinctive handicap in terms of accent, pattern of behavior, or physical appearance. There are indications that as long as the Iranian immigrants remain as a group without a community or fail to maintain their direct ties with the homeland, their children will have an identity without its Iranian cultural content and as a group they will become more and more English speaking. In that case, the assimilation of Iranian immigrants in the United States appears to be a matter of a few years and not one or two generations. Moreover, it seems that the Iranian immigrants' pattern of behavior regarding socialization of their children confirms Gordon's assertion that all people belonging to a social class are likely to act alike and to have similar values, even if they have different ethnic backgrounds.[3]

REACTIONS OF PARENTS

The data show that, despite the common marginal experience, two types of family lifestyles seem prevalent among first-generation Iranians. Each displays a distinct reaction to the character training of their children.[4] One type represents what we may call Iranian-directed parents, who at the present time appear to be more representative of the majority of first-generation Iranian parents. In a sense, the actual situation of this type of Iranian family is that of marginality at cultural and social-psychological levels. That is, they are conscious of themselves as "Khareji" (aliens) and identify themselves by referring to Iran and the Iranian value system.

The major characteristics of Iranians-directed parents is that they are highly conscious of their traditional parental role, thinking of themselves as Iranian in a way in which they had never thought in Iran. Thus, when it comes to child socialization they express a strong desire to cultivate the "positive" aspects of their culture. Among the members of this group interpersonal relationship with the children remains strongly colored by Iranian behavioral patterns. For example, they are most likely to predominant importance to the child's compliance with parental authority, especially the father, even though independence and individuality are stressed.

Responding to a question, "How concerned are you with providing your children with an understanding of the Iranian culture?" almost all the parents state that they have been very concerned. In a response to another question inquiring into what the parents have done in regard to transmitting Iranian identity, we find that the overwhelming majority answer in terms of "speaking Farsi in the home at all times," constantly reminding my child that you are not American, you are Iranian born in the United States," or "sending my wife and the children to Iran every summer." When these parents specify the kind of Iranianness they have in mind, their focus is generally on language and not on other spheres such as religious observance. For example, only two couples had taken their children to visit a mosque. Although all the respondents are very much concerned that their children speak Farsi, there is a sense of disappointment that they are unable to counteract the Americanization process. As the following remarks indicate, most of the parents are anguished about the Americanization of their children.

> The second generation is a lost generation. Some of our offspring are ashamed to bear non-American names. They are uprooted. We have been deprived of the chance to raise the kind of children we wanted to. I am a devoted Iranian, but my children seldom act like Iranians.

A common concern voiced by those parents who have only school-age children is the stressful impact of their children on their lives,

> The responsibility and burden of being a real Iranian parent is enormous.
>
> The American way of life separates our children from us.
>
> Most Iranians will face great problems when they have teenagers.
>
> I constantly tell my son that we did not return to Iran because of his future.
>
> Unfortunately all he knows as an Iranian is that his parents come from Iran.

An Iranian father is scornful of the apathy shown by some Iranian couples.

> They are insensitive to the Iranian heritage. They choose American-sounding names for their children.

One fifty-year-old physician frankly says:

> It is our fault that our children grow up without any sense of cultural background. We usually become involved in our professions so that we miss the chance of raising our children as Iranian-American. I have known of several Iranian families in which Americanization of children caused family disintegration. It is not the children's fault. We raised them as American children, so now we should not expect them to be un-American.

As these statements indicate, the nearly universal desire of the parents to transmit Iranian culture contrasts with the child's objective upbringing settings. The second-generation Iranian, although raised within the Iranian family in which Farsi is the language, has no roots in the parents' past, consequently has only the future toward which to look.

A second type of first-generation Iranian parent is the American-directed parent, or what is called the Persian Yankee. This type includes a sizable number of Iranian-American couples. In general, they maintain a status consciousness rather than an ethnic consciousness. Most of these families display what Irvin Child called "the rebel reaction." It involves a predominance in the individual of the motive to achieve complete acceptance by the American group.

With regard to the children's socialization, they have accepted their Americanization as unavoidable and to some extent desirable. They have come to the realization that dealing with conflicting cultures "creates barriers for the children to enter into the mainstream of American society." As several parents stated: "our children have no future in Iran; it is better for them to grow up as American and feel American." In this type of family, the children's social behavior is not different from that of the third generation of American immigrants. For instance, "When we have a guest at home, he does not join us; or they want to have their own privacy."

Moreover, some have no Iranian names, and almost all have no understanding of Farsi. The issue of identity confusion was raised by several parents. "I asked my husband not to talk Farsi to my daughter, because it was so confusing for her," stated three non-Iranian wives.

Non-Iranian wives in this type of family have a stronger voice in regard to the children's socialization than the Iranian fathers. Such dominating positions are expressed in the following statements:

> I do not think I would like my son to grow up like his father, neither American nor fully Iranian.

> I would like my daughter to grow up with a sense of security and independence.

Over and over again in conversations with the parents, a dominant theme is the development of a child with a secure personality. As another stated, "I would like my daughter to be raised with personality" (a high level of personal security). Another non-Iranian mother pointed out, "I have repeatedly asked my husband not to set up his own childhood experience as an unquestionable model for our children."

The limited observations indicate that the Iranian father in these families remains a cultural stranger to the world of his children, and his interaction with them often results in misunderstanding and conflict. But, as expected, Iranian-American couples in general do not show the critical view of Iranian couples toward the assimilation of the children. They remind others that "our children are simply Americans, neither better nor worse, adjusted to the normal life of their own socioeconomic strata."

In short, Iranian immigrants have acculturated over one generation much as other immigrants have done over three generations. Moreover, while the majority of Iranian parents have been "very much concerned" about the ethnic identity of the children, most second-generation Iranians are alien to the culture of their parents, which is foreign in origin and not altogether comprehensible. The lack of an ethnic community, and greater exposure to the American culture and its way of life have undermined a devotion to Iranian cultural heritage. While the couples, particularly the Iranian couples, remain marginal people, their children grow up in one society and by one culture. It may safely be predicted that the second-generation Iranian will soon become structurally assimilated within the American society and will constitute an unaffiliated group. Unfortunately, the assimilation of the second-generation Iranian is taking place at a time when a renewed interest in ethnicity continues among the third-generation Americans.

CHAPTER 10

Conclusion

This study has been concerned with the problems and dilemmas which face a group of Iranian middle class immigrants in the United States. It has primarily focused on the inside world of the immigrants' community. An attempt was made to explain the immigrants' condition of dual marginality as it is perceived by the immigrants, to compare what the immigrant thinks with what he actually does, and, finally, to explain his response to his situation of dual marginality.

Some concluding observations may be made about the findings of this study. Before I proceed to do so, I must note that generalizations ought not to be made beyond the scope of this study as defined by the data.

The first general observation emerging from the study is connected with the characteristics of the immigrants' community. This community manifested peculiarities derived from its predominantly middle class, professional origin and from its uncertainty in an alien environment. In terms of immigrant settlement, it was found that the Iranian immigrants resemble the third generation of American immigrants. That is, due to the pattern and character of their migration as well as their occupational composition, they live in a geographical dispersion and have no distinguishable pattern of common locale. There is no Little Persia.

In terms of community as a social process of interaction, it was found that the Iranian community represents an inadequate institutional structure. That is, the existing we-feeling of the immigrants has not led to an interdependent feeling or to mutual obligations among themselves. Thus what exists is a community in process, characterized by a lack of supporting institutions and social cohesiveness. In such a community the immigrants live basically as individuals, or as a series of isolated families, with no significant and lasting mutual relationships. In this respect, the Iranian community in America continues to remain an integral part of its larger community at home—one which also lacks cohesiveness and unity. The community represents, moreover, its larger segment at home.

The members tend to emphasize their own personal interests and to avoid social commitment to others. Therefore, the community in which the immigrants live does not provide the environment for the growth of social potentialities which have been thwarted by the situation in Iran. Thus it does not satisfy the social desire which has been for many the determinant of immigration. In short, the Iranian community does not fit at all the traditional characterization of the ethnic group as a tightly knit community freed from past experience and released from the traditional constraints of the homeland. The forces which draw the immigrant away from his own group membership are considerably stronger than those which attract him toward in-group relations. That is, cultural and social factors have created barriers quite as effective as those of geographical dispersions as the formation of group cohesiveness.

Another general conclusion of this study is that the Iranian community proved to encompass a wider variety of types than is generally presumed. As the data indicated, despite a common situation of dual marginality the immigrants reacted to their situation through a variety of responses. Four distinctive responses were found. Among these was the so-called ambivalent Iranian; that category constituted the majority of the immigrants.

The ambivalent Iranian represents an ideal type of dually marginal man. Unlike the other three types, who, through various techniques, are capable of minimizing their marginality, the ambivalent Iranian still experiences a complete dual marginality. Because he has remained an undecided immigrant, he is more subject to a situation characterized by conflict, uncertainty, and alienation.

The dominant orientation of the ambivalent Iranian is a state of dual detachment from both home and host societies. He is caught between four or more social worlds: with a social-psychological uncertainty toward each of them, he knows he cannot accept any of the positions, either in Iran or in America, with his whole heart and with certainty.

This type of immigrant lives a marginal life in American society. He guards himself against conscious Americanization and does not extend his involvement beyond his family. His marginality, moreover, is accompanied by a considerable hostility and anti-Americanism, both of which stem from his own cultural conflicts. It is, in fact, this feeling of hostility and his belief in the impermanence of his residency which militate against his adjustment to the present situation. While the majority of the members of this group are seriously considering the idea of re-emigration, there are other individuals in the same group who are in the process of becoming settlers and who have given up the hope of returning to Iran.

Thus, as a community most undecided immigrants can be seen as "bast neshin," (unsettled passive resisters). This community is decidedly unlike an ethnic enclave in the process of structural assimilation. Its members remain oriented toward re-emigration and maintain their identification with their status community at home. Thus their present situation is characterized by a lack of stability in group ties and by the existence of status inconsistency. It appears that the tensions of uncertainty and dual marginality will continue until the undecided immigrant either gives up his idea of return and becomes a full-fledged immigrant or returns to Iran and remains there.

The majority of the immigrants in the other three types were found to be relatively well adjusted to their present situation. Their commitment to the role of national was found to be mellowing with the years, and to be diluting with professional, political, and practical Americanization. Whether this ongoing trend will become a dominant aspect in the life of these immigrants remains to be seen in the light of future socio-political changes in Iran and the prospect of the lack of economic opportunities in the United States.

In short, it is clear that the Iranian community continues to remain, although in America, an integral part of the larger Iranian society. Given but the material contained in this study, it would be extremely difficult to project the future of this community on these shores. That is, it is still too early to forecast the direction in which the Iranian community in America will be moving in its response to the changing situation in both countries.

EPILOGUE

Continuity and Change 1985

EPILOGUE

Continuity and Change—1985

Iranians in the United States and the 1979 Islamic Revolution

Since the completion of data gathering for this study a historically unique event has taken place in Iran. For whatever one's view of the Islamic revolution in Iran, one cannot deny that an event of lasting historic significance has taken place, which has, indeed, underlined the oppositional potential of Shiism and the importance of its political implications. In so far as the revolution ousted the Pahlavi dynasty, displaced the ruling elite directly associated with it, and established itself as an Islamic Republic, it drastically changed the pattern and the nature of Iranian emigration to the United States. Consequently, the Iranian community in the United States has since undergone important changes in its character, its social composition and, notably, its political orientation.

The different currents of change which are still unfolding in the Iranian community in the United States may be summarized as follows:

A New Kind of Emigrant

Most societies have had their exodus, refugees, and displaced people during periods of deep crisis and confused historical moment. The Iranian revolution, a truly grass-root movement which involved revolt against Iran's dominant class and its entire value system, was no exception. During the course of revolution and after the establishment of the Islamic Republic, a large number of Iranians emigrated to the United States. The arrival of the post-revolutionary sojourners and political refugees opened an entirely new chapter in the history of Iranians in America. What was once basically an emigration of limited number of non-returnee students, is now predominantly an emigration of a relatively large number of middle and upper class Iranian families.

The new pattern of emigration is complex in quality, motivation, and quantity. In terms of quality, it is heterogeneous in social biography, religious affiliation, (e.g., Jews, Christians, and Bahai's), political attitudes and age. In terms of professional training it is composed of scientists, college professors, physicians, managers, former army officers, nurses, artists, engineers, filmmakers, journalists, entrepreneurs, and particularly from the Jewish community in Iran, the businessmen.

In terms of political orientation, it includes sympathizers with the old regime and post-revolutionary alienated intellectuals, both Marxist and non-Marxist activists. It seems that a combination of political, professional, and religious marginality have produced a "vocabulary of motive" for emigration of newcomers to the United States. Thus, they have managed to escape the compound crisis of being disenchanted intellectuals, rejected Westernized professionals, and the powerless affluent. In addition to those individuals who emigrated for reasons of personal and economic security, the extreme uncertainty over the new governments' stand on religious diversity and private enterprise led many of Iranian Jews and Bahai's to leave the country during the period immediately before and after the Iranian revolution. Of all the non-Muslim minorities, Bahai's found themselves the most vulnerable, because just as in the Western-based constitution of 1906, in the new constitution they were not considered as followers of a religion, but rather as heretics of Shiism.

In terms of quantity, the exact number of newcomers is unknown. An indicator of the political orientation of this group, however, is the number admitted to the United States as political refugees. During the three-year period from 1982 to March 1985, 18,139 persons born in Iran have requested asylum in the United States; of this group, 11,055 have been granted political asylum.[1] Estimates of the total number—both old permanent immigrants and recent immigrants—vary from 500,000 to 800,000. My data at this stage are incomplete, and more information is required to give a statistical description of the newcomers. Scattered data suggest that the newcomers may be found in all major cities, but the great bulk of them are now residing in California and New York. For instance, according to a newly published report, in 1970 only 20,000 Iranians lived in Los Angeles. Today's colony is over 200,000.[2]

National Revival

The revolutionary movement of 1978-79 gave rise to a sense of national revival among the Iranians in the United States. During the period of uprising in Iran, Iranians in the United States, regardless of their political orientation, came together as a national group, and the community as a whole became an outpost of the Iranian Revolution. In addition, to those Iranians who remained active in anti-Shah demonstrations here, some of the political activists who considered themselves exiles from the Pahlavi regime, returned to Iran and took active roles in the revolutionary movement.

Moreover, the extensive coverage of anti-Shah demonstrations by the mass media served to shatter the illusions of Americans, who had been ignorant of "the other Iran." Their sudden awareness provided a convicing argument for the major reason for Iranian involuntary emigration in the last twenty-five years. The American public had learned at last of a situation initially caused by United States support of a highly unpopular regime in Iran since the early 1950s.

Religious Identity

Another consequence of the Islamic movement in Iran is a newly developed sense of religious cohesiveness among a segment of Iranian Muslims in the United States. The Islamic movement not only captured the imagination of the masses in Iran; it also fueled a resurgence of Islam among Iranians in this country. In the last few years several Islamic Centers and mosques have been established in certain areas such as New York, Washington, D.C., Maryland, and California. Today the mosque has become the most important cultural institution in the Iranian religious community. Religious Iranians look upon these centers as a means of preserving their religious identity and also as a way of eliminating the damaging influences of American culture, especially the emphasis on material things upon the second-generation. The Islamic Centers have had a deep impact upon religious Iranians, as a Muslim community *ummat* and as individuals. The weekly gatherings for religious discussions and Quran reading, mourning on the death day of various Imams, celebration of their birth, the gatherings for weddings and death, and most important, the Friday prayers observed in these mosques—all indicate a new sense of religious cohesiveness.

Emerging New Organizations

The newcomers have already begun to have a visible cultural, political, and economic impact on the cities where they have settled in sizable numbers. For instance, it is reported that in the Beverly Hills elementary schools one in six children is Iranian.[3] Presumably, the bulk of the Iranian population in California alone is so great that since 1981 the Iranian Directory Yellow Pages has been published by an Iranian corporation, Ketab Corporation. This directory is delivered free of charge to Iranian community residents, businesses, and institutions. The 1983 addition is 330 pages, contains all kinds of advertisements in the following varied goods and services: travel, skin care, food production, driving school, auto care, Persian rugs, banking, insurance, medical and plastic surgery, restaurants, night clubs. All are owned and operated by Iranians. In addition, more than seventeen Iranian associations and centers, most of them non-existent seven years ago, are listed in this edition.

With regard to community supportive institutions, the rate of change is such that I find novel organizations with no parallel in the past. Today there are a great number of newspapers and journals aimed at the Iranian Community in the United States. In addition, there are radio and TV broadcasts in Farsi in some of the major cities. In these programs a powerful effort has been made to revive Iranian cultural awareness, emphasizing community cohesiveness, native language, and pursuit of business affairs and political claims. However, the predominant theme of the broadcasting for instance, in New York City, is that of eventual return to Iran. In this respect, the newcomers display the very same ambivalence as did the Iranians of the 1970s, whom we have characterized by their showing intense nostalgia towards the home society.

Another novel development is the establishment of several Farsi language programs. As the immigrant press indicates, there are several Farsi classes in New York, Washington D.C., Virginia (Arlington), and California. If these Farsi classes survive and interest and participation increase, the second-generation Iranians will grow up with at least some understanding of their ethnic language, though they might become culturally assimilated in American society.

The nourishing of the Iranian organizations in the United States is perhaps an accurate reflection of their ethnic consciousness—the yearning for maintaining group identity, for the familiar pleasures and the simple desire not to be alone among strangers. But at the same time it reflects their wealth, their patterns of consumption, and their readjustment to the new environment.

Emerging Anti-Iranian Reaction

During the hostage crisis (November 1979 to January 1981) Iran and Iranians were in the headlines, and this provoked considerable anti-Iranian reaction among native Americans, a feeling almost non-existent in the mid-1970s. In a manner reminiscent of the experiences of Japanese Americans in the 1940s, Iranians in the United States became scapegoats and suffered harassment and covert discrimination, mainly because of their national heritage. The anti-Iranian reaction was so widespread that it forced Iranian-Americans to misrepresent their ethnic identity. Such experience, which has several parallels in the history of immigrants in the United States, made Iranian-Americans aware that no matter how Americanized they may be, they are considered by the native-born Americans as aliens.

Declining Professional Representation

Two important factors seem to have a great impact upon the professional representation of the Iranian community in the United States. One is a Federal law which was passed in January, 1977. Under this law the recruiting of foreign interns and residents in the United States was to be stopped by 1980. The implication of this law for the Iranian community is that the number of Iranian physicians in the United States will no longer increase.

The second factor is the decline of Iranian student enrollment in American colleges and universities. According to the latest survey published by the Institute of International Education, only 35,860 Iranians attended college in the 1982 academic year. The survey shows a steady decline from a record high of 51,870 in 1980 through 47,550 in 1981. Obviously, the reduction of Iranian students in the United States will also have some impact upon the professional characteristics of the community. As the data in this book indicate, a large proportion of Iranian professional immigrants initially came with the student visa and eventually changed their status to that of permanent immigrants.

In short, as all these recent developments indicate, the Iranian community since 1978 has undergone some important qualitative and quantitative changes. Little Persia, the phenomenon of the Iranian neighborhood, is emerging in certain areas such as Queens in New York and Beverly Hilts in Los Angeles. Scattered data suggest that an increasing number of the pre-revolutionary immigrants have been naturalized or are applying for citizenship. For the first time the Iranian immigrant, the one who has realized that he cannot go back home, publically admits that he is a citizen of the United States.[4] White the pre-revolutionary immigrants gradually give up the hope of returning to Iran, and become marginal to their marginal groups, the newcomers become the new dually marginal Iranians who remain up to a point "uncertain" immigrants. Both situations, at home and abroad, contain for them some elements of uncertainty, non-belonging and insecurity. Of course, at the present time, the "mission" orientation of the newcomer as a political refugee remains a strong organizational principle, and in this respect he differs from the prerevolutionary Iranian immigrant. The pro-monarchy exites resemble in some respects those Cuban refugees who came to the United States with the hope of someday overthrowing the Castro regime and returning to Cuba. Among the political refugees, the post-revolutionary alienated intellectuals are the most disenchanted of the Iranian immigrants. Considering themselves former dedicated revolutionaries who participated in the Iranian revolution, and having hoped to remold their society after their own political image, they now find themselves in a situation of dual and compounded uprootedness. The fact that these individuals now have taken refuge in America has created a repeated situation peculiar to the history of Iranian emigration to the United States. It reminds us of those involuntary immigrants in this study who had chosen their erstwhile enemy as their host.

The question remains as to how the Iranian community in general will readjust itself to the new conditions. In a community as hopelessly divided and fragmented as the Iranian, how wilt new different groups respond to the anguish of uprootedness and marginality? What is happening is only the working out of a process that started three decades ago.

PART III

The Making of the Iranian Community in America 1985-1990

PART III

The Making of the Iranian Community in America[1]

Introduction

The Iranian revolution of 1979 was both culturally and organizationally crucial to the making of the Iranian community in the United States. It is ironic that while the tragedy of American Iranian relations was still unfolding, a new secular "Iran" inside America was growing increasingly Americanized and rapidly asserting itself as a high status ethnic community. Today, as the nation of Iran is passing through its own critical historical moments, Iranian-Americans are also making their own history, but not quite under conditions of their choosing. Herein lies the supreme irony of the closing decade of America's post-World War II imperial claim over Iran; Iran's loss ultimately turned out to be America's gain.

Emigration from Iran to the United States is a recent phenomenon and became significant only in the early 1980s. It occurred during two phases. The first phase started in the 1950s and lasted until 1977. During this period Iranians came often as sojourners and temporary migrants (students, interns), but eventually changed their status to permanent residents. During the peak period (1842-1903) of immigration to the United States, only 130 Iranian nationals were known to have entered America. However, starting in 1945 emigration from Iran rose steadily and in 1966 exceeded 1,200 per year. A peak was reached in 1972 with 3,059 immigrants. The number of non immigrants (visitors, student interns, and so on) increased drastically from an annual average of about 1,400 in the 1950s to 6,000 in the 1960s, reaching the highest figure of 98,018 in 1977. However, during the same period, a total of only 34,855 Iranian immigrants were admitted, and 8,877 became naturalized U.S. citizens (Bozorgmehr and Sabbagh, 1988).

It is particularly notable that the pattern of Iranian migration during this period did not involve "chain migration;" it was basically an individual and not the whole family migration. For the most part, it involved highly intellectual and professional groups (physicians, dentists, scientists, engineeers and so on). For example, from 1962 to 1969 Iran lost about 400 physicians and 10,000 other professionals to America (Immigration and Naturalization Services, 1953-1973). In the mid-1970s, 2,373 physicians of Iranian origin were on the rolls of the American Medical Association.

The majority of these immigrant professionals had voluntarily chosen migration as a response to their political, social, and professional marginality in Iran. Once in the United States, their feelings of marginality or alienation coexisted with the experience of cultural estrangement. As Everett Stonequist once observed, "The individual who has emigrated from the higher classes of a nationality with a proud and self-conscious history finds it especially difficult to identify himself with the new country" (Stonequist, 1937: 88). As a result, a tendency toward re-emigration was one of the main characteristics of this higher class Iranian immigrant. Although no accurate official estimates are available regarding the re-emigration of Iranian professionals during and after the 1979 Revoluation. Evidently, a relatively sizable numbers of American-trained returnees now live in Iran.

The second phase of Iranian migration began from 1978 to 1980, during the period immediately before and after the Iranian revolution. In ousting the Pahlavi dynasty, displacing the ruling class directly associated with it, and establishing an Islamic Republic, the revolution drastically changed the pattern and the nature of Iranian migration. What was once basically an emigration of a limited number of non-returnee professionals became predominantly an emigration of a relatively large number of middle and upper class Iranian families.

More Iranians live in the United States today than in any other country in the world except Iran. Estimates of the size of the Iranian-American population varies, with some sources claiming the number exceeds 500,000. We shall have to await the results of the 1990 census to determine the precise figure. In terms of geographical distribution, Iranians reside in and around the nation's major urban areas in the far west and northeast. According to the 1980 census, almost 50 percent of the Iranian-born live in California, particularly in Los Angeles. The second largest concentration of Iranians is in New York and New Jersey; the third largest is in the District of Columbia, Virginia, and Maryland areas.

Because it consists of a large number of professionals, entrepreneurs, and store owners, the contemporary Iranian community in America is an ethnic community of a special kind. Perhaps uniquely among ethnic communities, professionals comprise the largest occupational category of Iranians outside of Iran. Of course, in their essentially involuntary emigration, dual marginality, and acculturation experience, Iranian Americans have much in common with other immigrant groups. But, the Iranian emigration also differs sharply from others in its pattern and nature. The pre-revolutionary Iranian emigration was one of highly professional and technical Iranian people to the United States. The post-revolutionary emigration also involved predominantly professionals but also involved the movement of a considerable amount of capital. No one knows exactly how much money Iranians brought to the United States, but estimates range between 30 and 40 billion dollars. The so-called money refugees from Iran have perhaps made greater investments than any other ethnic group in America. My data at this stage are incomplete, but random conversations both with the American lawyers of Iranian clients and with informed Iranians suggest that a sizable portion of the 1979-80 real estate boom in the Los Angeles region resulted from the investment capital of Iranian immigrants.

For these so-called money refugees who settled in the United States there is no success like exile. Today, they are most likely naturalized Americans and have established themselves as big real estate owners, bankers and financeers. In fact, it did not take long before certain expensive areas in Beverly Hills, Santa Monica, San Francisco and Orange County were identified by the local residents as "Persian Hills" or "Iranian Mansions" and "Irangeles." More importantly, a significant number of these super rich Iranian Americans have become top-notch entrepreneurs in American high finance. Others with more modest wealth invested their money into businesses such as construction firms, textile and clothing outlets, rug stores, jewerly stores, gas stations, used car services, and restaurants.

Wherever the rich Iranian immigrants live in America today, they are the most visible examples of Iran's big spenders newly rich. They wasted little time in achieving the same success that they had enjoyed in Iran. Generally, present-day Iranian businessmen in the United States appear more adventurous, aggressive and profit-motivated than their predecessors. Soon after settling, they injected new dynamism into local economies. In Los Angeles, for instance, their economic and cultural influence far outweigh their numbers. In addition to the major department stores and shopping centers owned by several wealthy families, over 50 Iranian-owned stores and restaurants are centured in one rich area, the Westwood Boulevard called "Irangeles."

Whether they reside in Los Angeles, Seattle, Houston, Washington, D. C., New York, or New Jersey, these Iranian-Americans tend to be the most influential foreign-born businessmen in their community. In Secaucus, New Jersey, in a newly built plaza called the Oriental Rug Industry Center of America, the majority of rug wholesalers and importers are Iranian-Americans. Although some of these have been rug dealers since the 1950s, they have been joined in the business by a large number of younger Iranian-American entrepreneurs who are highly educated and definitely upscale. Moreover, there are scores of Iranian-owned oriental rug stores and showrooms in every major city in America. In the District of Columbia, Virginia, and Maryland alone, an estimated 300 rug stores are owned by Iranians.

From the very beginning, the Iranian immigrants differed from other arrivals by their high educational and professional achievements. The 1980 census indicated that only about 4 percent of Iranians did not go beyond the eighth grade as compared to 32.9 percent for all immigrants and 16.7 percent for natives. With regard to a graduate university education, about 23 percent of Iranians had a graduate degree as compared to 12.5 percent for the foreign-born and 7.5 percent for natives (Bozorgmehr & Sabbagh, 1988). It must be noted that the census counted only 121,505 Iranians in the United States, including citizens, permanent residents, students and even visitors. Furthermore, the census was taken just 44 months after the revolution and, therefore, did not include over 300,000 Iranians, mostly professionals, who subsequently arrived. An occupational profile, compiled as part of the census, revealed that 24 percent of Iranians in the United States were professionals, double the proportion of the native-born and the foreign-born as a whole. A survey of 450 Iranian-American residents in the northern part of New Jersey revealed that 86 percent were professionals and managers, as opposed to about 24 percent for the total American population. A breakdown of membership in the Society of Iranian Professionals in the county of Santa Clara shows that out of 405 members, about 140 are college graduates and over 235 have M.A. and Ph.D. degrees.

Today, American trained professionals such as physicians, college professors, scientists, dentists, nurses, engineers, and managers comprise the largest occupational segment of Iranian-Americans. Until the late 1970s, the Iranian professionals in the United States were over-represented by physicians. A study of foreign medical graduates in the United States (Marguleim, 1969:80) reveals that the United States has approximately one Iranian medical graduate for every five at home. Iranian-American physicians may be found in all major cities, but the great bulk of them now reside in California, New York, and New Jersey. They constitute a self-conscious status community in the Iranian-American community. It is, in fact, a community within a community. Its members share mobility, aspirations, consumption norms, private schooling for their children, and leisure-time activities. Moreover, as the most Americanized Iranians, they choose to limit their social contacts to their own status group. The medical education for those who are the only foreign-educated members of their families has resulted in upward mobility. Some of these individuals experience marginality to their own ethnic community and to the host society. It seems that the situation of this type of immigrant resembles that of "secret marginality," formulated by David Riesman. He or she usually does not share the marginality of other Iranians but remains marginal to the marginal group. Iranian-American physicians have done relatively well, often achieving upper middle class positions in less than two decades. In addition to over 3,000 Iranian born physicians listed by the American Medical Association, thousands of post-revolutionary professionals are now employed by corporations, educational institutions and hospitals. An unestimated number of experienced Iranian engineers also hold top positons in IBM, AT&T, Boeing and oil refineries in Houston.

*The field work on which this study is based was carried out during 1985-1989. The data was primarily gathered through participation and interviews with over 400 Iranians in Los Angeles, Seattle, Washington, D.C., New York and New Jersey. As a director of Persian language program, I have also observed over 30 second generation teenage Iranians every Saturday for two hours, the last three years.

CHAPTER 11

Community Structure

Since the Iranian revolution in 1978, Iranians in the United States have grown from a scattered, ambivalent immigrant group of perhaps 80,000 permanent residents and students into an ethnic community of over 400,000 persons, concentrated in "Little Irans." These new ethnic communities are based on both cultural symbols as well as modern and rational considerations. Iranian immigrants belong to a generation of upwardly mobile, secularized cosmopolitans. Unlike the "tired and poor," uneducated refugees of Gemeinschaft-type communities, Iranians are professionals, entrepreneurs, well traveled, and bilingual. Therefore, the contents of their cultural baggage often include American educational degrees, professional licenses, checkbooks, credit cards, an international driver's license and (in the case of absentee American "permanent residents," an expired American driver's license and social security ID), a copy of the *Rubaivat* of Omar Khayyam, the *shahnameh* (the Persian national epic completed about 1000 A.D.), a piece of Persian miniature, a *Koran* (if he or she is a *moslem*), cans of golden caviar and most definitely packages of Persian pistachio and saffron. Some Persian luxury articles, such as Persian rugs (Kashan or Kerman made) and other handicraft essentials to decorate his or her Persian room here in America, are usually sent separately. All of these material cultural items are either man made symbols of a unique cultural inheritance or by-products of Iranian westernization—some say over-westernization—and its Western-educated middle classes.

These new immigrants are indeed ethnic, but they do not live within the traditional communities that are typically based on intense, face-to-face, significant and lasting relationships. They were born and raised in an environment in which their traditional cultural patterns were already undermined. Thus, their communal relationships lack territorial identity and *Gemeinschaft* relationships. As high status ethnics, they don't need their own colony to function as a bridge of transition or as a halfway house on the road to assimilation.

This is not to suggest that Iranians in the United States are already structurally assimilated and will soon disappear as Iranians.

Indeed, Iranians have just started to create their own communal structure and are displaying a renewed interest in their ethnicity. But, as Max Weber emphasized, the ethnic community itself is not a community; it facilitates types of communal relationships (Ethnic Groups, 1968). In this sense Iranians are creating their own community. Ironically, even though their new communal associations are rationally constructed and bureaucratically managed, they respond to the emotional needs of the vast majority of Iranians in America who are dually marginal. The dialectically interrelated anti-western action in Iran and anti-Iranian reaction in America not only transferred the already available marginal identity to a much larger group, but also reinforced the development of a new community.

Each category of new Iranian immigrants brought into the United States distinctive abilities and political orientations, and each is currently undergoing a distinctive process of adjustment. Perhaps the major element they have in common was they they were all forced to leave Iran. That is, they came for reasons that involved their middle-class life styles and their political, professional, and religious marginality in Iran. For most Iranian intelligentsia, post-revolutionary Iranian society no longer offered a viable living alternative. Ironically, here in exile, they keep wishing for an Iran that no longer exists.

The basic difference between today's situation and that of the pre-revolutionary period is that the post-revolutionary political immigrants have a "mission" orientation. However, having remained hopelessly divided and disenchanted, the mission orientation has functioned as a strong organizational element in exile. As the most conscious cultural agents of Iran, the intelligentsia have become the leading figure in establishing the culturally distinctive institutions of the Iranian-American community. The last five years have witnessed a remarkable cultural flowering of an essentially persian character. For example, the number of newspapers and periodicals aimed at the Iranian community is very impressive. Five daily newspapers, three magazines, and over ten monthly journals are published in Los Angeles alone. In fact, there are more Iranian newspapers per capita in America than in Iran. In addition, there are over thirty radio and ten television broadcasts in Persian in some of the nation's metropolitan areas.

The Iranian communities in America are not based on traditional foundations but on new institutions and forms of association that can be found in the urban, bureaucratic American context. For many Iranian immigrants, these new associations or renovated cultural symbols provide sources for expressing their ethnic identity.

Since the second-generation Iranian is rapidly Americanizing, all these institutions in their present content and form will probably only last for one generation. For now, however, they constitute the functional equivalent of the myths, values, and familiarities in which the traditional immigrant identify and community were grounded.

In the case of Iranian-Americans, these institutional supports include:

— the Iranian Directory Yellow Pages
— Farsi Media
— Persian Language Programs
— Anjomans (Cultural Association)
— Now-ruz (spring festival)
— Dowreh (informal gathering)
— Professional Associations
— Electronic Community
— Shab-i shear (poetry reading night)
— Persian music
— Khaneghah (Sufi Center)
— Masjid (Mosque)

The Iranian Directory Yellow Pages

Ethnic identity in a new country is maintained in various ways. The Iranian community manifests peculiarities derived from its predominantly professional origin, business class and geographical dispersion. The *Iranian Directory Yellow Pages* is perhaps the best evidence of a rational, formalized community structure. The establishment of the directory paralleled the arrival of the post-revolutionary Iranian immigrants in America. It was first published in January 1981 in Los Angeles by a young civil engineer. Today there are five *Iranian Directory Yellow Pages* published in the United States: Eastern U. S. (New York, New Jersey, Connecticut); northern California; southern California; Houston, Texas; and Atlanta, Georgia. The directories, with tens of thousands of listings, are delivered free of charge to Iranian community residents and businesses. Each directory covers the entire nonterritorial professional and business community in the area.

Ketab Corporation, the publisher of the Southern California Directory, the largest one, is more than just a publisher. It also owns one of the few Farsi bookstores in America. The bookstore is located on Westwood Boulevard in Los Angeles, and is a focal point of the Iranian community. It addition, since 1987, Ketab Corporation has established the only Iranian information center in America. It is called 08 Center and is a twenty-four hour service. The code "08" is the Farsi version of Tehran's old telephone information center. A toll-free call will provide information about businesses and services, cultural and social events in town, books, writers and poets, and welfare and humanitarian agencies. Since 1980 its Yellow Pages have created not only an Iranian version of Bazaare (the word *bazaar* is a Farsi word meaning "traditional market"), but also a media identity for the Iranian occupational community.

However, a sociological analysis of the organizational culture of this Iranian marketing firm reveals some distinctive cultural features, perhaps the most distinctive of which is its quick success in becoming accepted as trustworthy. This is especially significant considering the feelings of insecurity and suspicion that Iranian immigrants brought with them from an oppressive society. In the Iranian community, where most people preferred to be known only by their first names and previously gave no information to any institution, Ketab has succeeded in gaining the people's trust.

Farsi Media

The Farsi mass media include newspapers, magazines, radio, television, monthly journals, and books. All are in the Farsi language, except for two journals printed in English.

Today there are a great number of newspapers and magazines aimed at the Iranian community. For example, five daily newspapers, three magazines, and over ten monthly journals are published in Los Angeles. In fact, there are more Iranian newspapers per capita in America than in Iran. In addition, there are over twenty radio and ten television braodcasts in Farsi in some of the nations' metropolitan areas. Book publishing in Farsi is also a growing phenomenon in America. In 1989 alone, over twenty new books in Farsi and ten books in English have been advertised and reviewed by the Iranian newspapers. Out of the thirty books published, twenty were published and even distributed by the authors themselves.

It is important to stress that the Farsi media in the United States is basically a media in exile because a large number of media people emigrated from Iran since the revolution of 1979. Thus, it lacks the historical development of starting as an immigrant media and growing into an American ethnic media. In most cases, these are the same newspapers and magazines that were banned under Iran's Islamic Republic. Just as the Iranian community primarily consists of Iranian-born members with interests and needs of high status immigrants, so its media is also owned and managed by those individuals who were born and trained in Iran.

To the inside observer, the Farsi media appears to be involved so completely with immigrants' political concerns that it shows no signs of deculturation. Many of the current publications are edited by Iranian-born editors who maintain a mission orientation and appeal to a more unassimilated reader. These politically oriented media, particularly those that are affiliated with major political groups, are losing their audiences and readership. On the one hand, the exile community is becoming politically frustrated and resigned; on the other hand, the Iranian community in general is becoming a younger and, consequently, primarily an English-speaking community. Indeed, the greatest threat to the Farsi media is the erosion of Farsi language among Iranians in America.

Depite these structural strains, the Farsi media plays a major role in creating an ingroup feeling among Iranians, particularly the post-revolutionary immigrants. In the absence of any other supportive institution to serve as an ethnic center, the Farsi media provides the primary component of Iranian identity. Furthermore, to a significant degree, its Farsi language functions as the only symbolic vehicle for entertainment among Iranians scattered throughout the country.

In fact, newspaper readership in the Iranian community is actually declining in contrast with the increase in the Iranian population in America. Despite the fact that the post revolutionary immigrants brought their own media to the United States, the Iranian community in general is a consumer of the American media. Two factors appear to be involved in this declining interest. First, the Farsi media in America reflect the circumstances of the Iranian community. They maintain an outsider position and represent their own factional ideas and political agenda. Second, the American context offers far greater competition for everyone's leisure time and energies. The English language press, radio and TV broadcasts, high frequency of long distance calls, and the increasing American media's coverage of Iranian affairs all compete for the Iranian's attention in America.

Persian Language Programs

Another novel development that serves to mark a sense of Persian identity and community is the establishment of Persian language programs. As the immigrant press indicates, there are now Persian classes in every area in which Iranian Americans reside. Most Iranian American parents are bilingual; some even speak other languages such as French and German. Their children, however, only speak English. Thus, the teaching of Persian as the primary means of preserving their cultural heritage has become a major concern of most Iranian American parents.

Anjomans

Since 1980 a large number of *Anjomans* (associations) have been established that relate directly to the revolution in Iran. From the very beginning of organized Iranian life in America to the 1979 revolution in Iran, the Iranian Student Association (founded in 1953) was the only organization of Iranians in the United States. Involved in anti-Iranian government activities, it did not appeal to the large non-political community. Not until the revolutionary movement of 1978-79 did the ISA bring Iranians in America together as it became an outpost of the Iranian revolution.

Iranian Americans tend to participate most actively in cultural associations. In a highly politicized and hopelessly divided community, the cultural associations with their non political, non religious character, and, more importantly, with their democratic bylaws, have a capacity to attract the majority of Iranians regardless of their political orientations and religious affiliations.

A telling sign of growing cohesion and solidarity among Iranians in the United States is the number of new Anjomans, most of them non-existent eight years ago. Today, almost no American city lacks its quota of Iranian American cultural associations.

These organizations, which are the basic organizational entity of the Iranian immigrants, are nonpolitical and nonreligious. They embrace all the Iranians in the area and provide resources for the expression of their ethnic identity. It is important to stress that these cultural associations respond essentially to the interests and needs of the Iranian immigrant. Lectures, social events, music, and even publications are in Farsi. Unlike other second-generation ethnic groups in America, second-generation Iranians are born into families in which the level of material wealth, the area of residence, and the pattern of consumption are much the same as that of professional Americans. Thus, greater exposure to the American culture and a physical proximity and social interaction with a large number of other Iranians have made the second-generation immigrants quite alien to their parents' cultural associations.

Now-ruz (Spring Festival)

"Now-ruz" is the only time that Iranians of all religions, regions, and ethnic groups come together as a national group. Now-ruz (pronounced no- ruze), the Iranian new year festival, is the greatest of the Persian feasts and celebrations. It is also the first day of spring—March 21, the vernal equinox—and has great cultural and national significance for Iranians.

As a spring rite, Now-ruz symbolizes all qualities of the season: rebirth, awakening, and the importance of family and friends. In popular Persian legend, Now-ruz was said to have been instituted by the mythical Persian king Jamshid. Now-ruz has a long history: When the Pilgrims celebrated the first Thanksgiving, Now-ruz had already been around for more than 2,000 years.

Preparations for this festival begin weeks before the new year actually arrives. Families plant wheat and lentil grains so they will sprout by Now-ruz. On New Year's Day itself, one should wear new clothes, exchange gifts, and visit relatives and friends. About an hour before the moment that signifies the arrival of spring, or Now-ruz, the family gathers around the "haft-seen."

The haft-seen is a table decorated with seven items, the names of which in Farsi begin with "seen" or the letter "s." Among the most popular are vinegar (serkeh); coin (sekeh); apple (sib); hyacinth (sounbol); garlic (seer); somag (a spice); samanu (a sweet wheat pudding); and senjed (a dried fruit from an Asian deciduous tree). In addition, there should be a plate of sabzi (greens), which usually consist of home-grown wheat sprouts or lentils. The table may also be decorated with a Qur'an, candle, and a goldfish in a bowl. These items are believed to bring happiness to every family during the new year.

The period of the Now-ruz festivities extends for two weeks. It begins on the last Wednesday of the outgoing year, called "Chahar-Shanbeh Souri," the Farsi term for Wednesday. The festivities continue until the thirteenth day of the new year (Sizdah Bedar—the Farsi word for thirteen). Since Iranians consider thirteen a symbol of bad luck, they counteract its evil by dwelling only on the good. Earth, air, and water are purifying elements that can ward off the evils of the thirteenth day of the new year. On the morning of this day, Iranians plan an outdoor picnic. They also take along the green sprouts grown for the haft-seen table and ceremoniously toss them into a stream of water.

For Iranian Americans, the spring festival, especially the Now-ruz celebration, is just as joyous a holiday in America as it ever was.

In fact, the Now-ruz festival is the only time that Iranian Americans come together as a national ethnic group. For all Iranians, no matter where they may be when the Now-ruz arrives, the most important part of the celebration is the reunion of family and friends. However, it is through the spectacular variety shows and New Year's Eve parties that an atmosphere of national identity is created.

More than fifteen major metropolitan areas hold Now-ruz parties with hundreds of guests in attendance. In New York, Los Angeles, and other major cities, other parties are sponsored by political activists and different Iranian religious minorities such as Iranian Jews and Zoroastrians. These separate parties illustrate the polarization of the Iranian community in America.

Dowreh (Informal Association)

"Dowreh" consists of an informal group of contemporaries and families who meet on a regular basis, rotating the meeting place among homes of members. Dowreh usually occurs during leisure time because the participants are occupationally heterogeneous.

Political dowrehs, which were composed of highly politicized elites, have played a major role in maintaining power positions among the political elite. In this context, dowreh is a functional equivalent of the political machine in urban America.

Dowreh is one of those cultural structures that Iranians have reconstructed in America. At the center of the Iranian community intimate primary groups significantly facilitate communal relationships over a great geographical distance. Furthermore, dowreh tends to transform the formal, impersonal and bureaucratic world into an informal and personal world. Unlike in Iran, dowreh in Iranian American communities is no longer an exclusive male gathering. In all known fifteen dowrehs in northern New Jersey, for example, males and females participate equally. Furthermore, just as the Iranian community is increasingly stratified in terms of occupations, so too are the dowrehs differentiated in terms of socioeconomic status.

Professional Associations

The increase in professional associations among Iranian Americans is remarkable, and has no parallel in the past. Since the idea of returning to Iran is no longer a dominating concern among most immigrants, they now typically believe that organizational affiliation is essential for an individual's advancement and adjustment.

In an earlier survey (1977), 90 percent of the respondents said they did not belong to any professional associations. No Iranian physicians, for example, indicated that they saw any need for an association of Iranian physicians in the United States. Today, over 3,000 Iranian physicians are members of the American Medical Association. About 90 percent of other professionals in the sample, such as scientists, engineers, and managers, are affiliated with different kinds of professional groups. In fact, because of the relative concentration of Iranian professionals in various institutions, they are becoming increasingly occupationally organized.

Presently, the most active professional organization is the Alumni Association of the Shiraz University School of Medicine in Iran. It holds annual meetings and sponsors a New Year's party in New York. At its 1989 annual meeting in Secaucus, New Jersey, it included two Farsi speakers discussing "cultural difficulties of Iranians in exile." No Farsi speaker was on the program at all for the 1988 meeting. This growing interest in becoming an ethnic American and accepting America as home is the working out of a process that was reinforced by the revolutionary movement of 1978-1979.

Electronic Community

Electronic linkages such as computer bulletin board, electronic mail exchanges, and newsgroups constitute an important means of association among the nationally and internationally dispensed Iranian community. They are made up of computers linked by telephone lines and equiped with software that allows them to dispatch and receive messages and information. Very large computer networks exist today, such as Internet, with an estimated two million members, and Usenet, with more than a million users, which form the backbone of an emerging international system (New York Times, November 13, 1990).

Iranians in the United States have found that the computer network offers a way to overcome the social isolation and lack of genuine communal relationships. Since March 1990 a group of Iranian scientists, engineers, and students residing in the United States have created their own electronic community, called Social, Culture Iranian. This newsgroup, like other ethnic newsgroups, is linked to one of the larger computer networks. The newsgroup was initiated by a group of Iranian-American scientists, most of whom had never met. In the last few months it has already attracted a large number of Iranian American professionals and scientists working in American universities and research institutions.

The Iranian electronic community in the United States consists of those Iranian-Americans who are self-conscious of their ethnic identity but know each other only electronically. For these Iranians, the Iranian newsgroup is a facinating and novel way to make contact and to comment on issues of shared concern. This is a new kind of non-spatial community that is unlimited by geography. Participants carry on extended discussions that can be read by other Iranians who may be located thousands of miles away. In addition to shrinking distances, the newsgroup also provides anonymity. These conditions lead to the expression of ideas that would rarely be expressed in face to face relationships. In a recent posting, for example, a survey was taken on the issue of Iranian female virginity. The concerned individual was asking "How many of you vote Yes or No for virginity?"

Members of the electronic community are encouraged to express their feelings and political ideologies. Those who are concerned for their safety and the safety of their families in Iran are advised to post their messages anonymously. In this context, there is a tendency for self-assertion by the participants. "Fear is what is keeping us from sharing our thoughts with each other" or "one of these days we all have to start fighting this fear instead of accomodating it." In this sense, the newsgroup reflects the distant and insecurity of the larger community of Iranians in the United States. Even though it is the most technologically advanced form of association, the electronic Iranian community has not achieved autonomy from its homeland culture.

Shab-i Shear (Poetry Reading Night)

Another transplanted cultural symbol that helps to maintain a sense of Iranian identity and community is the poetry reading night. Poetry for Iranians is more than just a form of expression; it is a medium and an essential feature of Iranian social life. Even illiterate Iranians know some poems by their great poets, such as Rumi, Khayyam, Sadi, Hafez, or Firdousi, the composer of the Persian national epic, the *Shahnameh.* There is hardly a Farsi newspaper that does not contain a poem from either these classical poets or the modern poets. In Iran, even city streets are named after poets.

Since 1980, some of the poets and writers in large cities such as Los Angeles, New York, and Washington, D. C., have recognized the necessity of organizing poetry reading sessions. At these gatherings poets of the Iranian diaspora have found a common cultural focal point. These institutionalized social settings draw large crowds of Iranian Americans from the surrounding area to listen to or read what these poets have created. These rather unique cultural events involve a great deal of intergroup communication as well as personal exchanges. Unlike the dowreh, the poetry reading night is not a closed association of a homogeneous group. It is open to everyone who is interested.

In the midst of the many competing claims for the individual's attention that are generated both within the Iranian community, and by the larger surrounding cultures, poetry and Persian music provides one of the few focuses that can draw Iranians together. Poetry also links Iranians with their lost homeland. In this context, the poetry reading both addresses and expresses the emigre's psychological needs and the fear that his/her ethnicity will be lost.

With regard to the Iranian Americans' situation of dual marginality—being marginal in the United States and also marginal at home—these social gatherings are quite self-satisfying and therapeutic. Consequently, national pride is never in short supply when Iranian poets congregate. As a result of their idealization of a "lost paradise," they can claim superiority to the rational structure of American society. This in turn makes for a more ambivalent relationship with the present realities of capitalism and materialism.

Persian Music

Another integrating feature of the Iranian American community is Persian music. Iran has a great musical tradition, closely linked to poetry and mysticism. Yet, after the 1979 revolution, the Iranian government banned music, viewing it as a means of promoting the decadent" culture of the West. At present, only certain types of music are allowed there, and anyone caught in possession of non-Persian music, such as pop music tapes, is treated as a criminal.

The forced emigration of Iranian musicians and singers added another important communal focus for Iranians in the United States. Today there are several centers whose purpose is to promote Iranian traditional music. In the absence of physical proximity, and more importantly, the lack of a religious organization, these cultural institutions provide the primary component of Iranian identity and, like poetry reading events, respond to the immigrant's psychological needs.

Khaneghah (Sufi Center)

"Sufi" is an Arabic word that applies to men and women who adopt an ascetic way of life. Sufiism was originally a practical faith, not a speculative and emotional religion. Early Sufis were closely attached to the Muslim religion but emphasized certain Qur'anic terms and verses. However, in principle, the kind of mystical knowledge represented by Sufiism has no place in Islam, because Allah, who is totally transcendental, can have no direct communication with man. Toward the end of the third century, Sufi mysticism became an organized system, with rules and a spiritual director. A sufi submitted himself absolutely to the spiritual director's guidance, as to one regarded as being in intimate communion with God.

A common saying is that "Sufiism" is the supreme manifestation of the Iranian mind in the religious sphere." Although not all Islamic mystics were Persians, with few exceptions the great poets of Iran adopted the Sufi's symbolic language. The doctrine of Iraniam Sufiism is illustrated in the celebrated "Mattnawi" of Jalal-Uddin Rumi. The depth of religious experience contained in Rumi's work is so great that "Mattnawi" is called the "Qur'an in Persia."

Among the Iranians in the United States, there is a large number of Sufi followers. "Khaneghah" (Sufi centers) exist today in New York, Washington, D.C., San Francisco, Los Angeles, Santa Cruz, Santa Fe, Seattle, and Chicago. Since 1987, a monthly journal published in London, in Farsi and English, has been distributed to all the U. S. Sufi Centers.

Mosque (Masjid)

Iranian Americans are religiously heterogeneous, and a majority of them are oriented toward a secular rather than religious outlook. Among the religious groups, the majority are Shiite Muslims. Other religious minority groups include Sunni, Jews, Christians, Zoroastrians, Bahai, and a variety of Sufi groups. It must be added that, under the Iranian constitution, Bahais are not considered as followers of a religion but rather as heretics of Shiism. Other religious minorities in Iran are granted legal recognition.

Since the Islamic revolution in Iran, a remarkable religious cohesiveness has developed among a segment of the Iranian Shiite Muslims. This revival, unprecedented in the Iranian community, is today an integrated part of the wider movement of Islam in America. Islam is one of the fastest growing religions in the United States, its numbers now exceeding 4.6 million. With higher rates of immigration and birth, together with the significant growth of Muslims among African Americans, American Muslims may surpass the the number of American Jews by 2010 (*New York Times*, 1989).

Paralleling the increase in American Muslims has been the tremendous expansion of *masjid* (mosques), particularly in New York City, New Jersey, Chicago, Detroit, Los Angeles and Toledo. About 600 mosques now exist in the United States, many in small buildings, former churches, converted stores, or even in renovated private homes. Multi-million dollar mosques were built in Los Angeles, New York City, and Washington, D.C. in the 1980s. These newly built mosques reflect Islamic architecture, with domes over their prayer areas and two minarets (about 135 feet high) on each side. Mosques are built in a way to face Mecca, Saudi Arabia, and Muslims are required to face it when they pray.

Although the majority of Muslims in the United States are not affiliated with a mosque, it is nonetheless a formidible institution, the most socially and politically active center in the Muslim community. The mosque is not only a house of worship; it has been the center of islamic learning, and a focus of political activity. Historically, the mosque has played an extremely important role in Islamic society. For example, Friday prayer, which takes place in a mosque, is an essentially political event. In Iran, even today, ten years after revolution, the vast network of mosques in every city or village play a uniquely political role. In the United States, there is one mosque in Brooklyn, New York, where young volunteers have set up a neighborhood patrol to fight drug pushers. But there are some muslim immigrants who feel a mosque is essentially a house of worship and, therefore, not an appropriate political headquarters or place for communal events such as weddings and funerals. (Y. Haddad, p. 51). Most of the mosques and Islamic centers in the United States contain multiracial and multiethnic Muslim groups. For example, the membership of two mosques in Paterson, New Jersey, consists of over 8 ethnic and racial groups. Thus, the Ummat (the Muslim community) manifests itself in terms of several national groups, providing for its members the comfort of a common cultural, linguistic and existential identity.

In addition to national and ethnic differences, there is the unending fued between Shiites and Sunnis. Since the Islamic revolution in Iran, this historical conflict has become more intense. Based on my personal observation of two large mosques in New York and New Jersey, the lack of joint social activities among Shiites and Sunnis outside of the mosque is attributed by Shiites to the assumed revolutionary nature of Shia Muslims as opposed to the conservatism of Sunni Islam. The radical/moderate division usually defined along Shia-Sunni lines is simplistics. Not all Shiites are radical. Thus, due to national differences, the Islamic brotherhood and sisterhood at the present time is a facade.

At the present time, Imam, the person who leads the congregation in the Friday prayer service is usually a bilingual man, communicating both in English and Arabic. Arabic is the language of prayer and sermons. The bilingual Imam is an outcome of Muslim immigration. It has been reported that mosque attenders are increasingly rejecting the use of Arabic in prayer and sermons (F. Reynolds and T. Ludwig, p. 117).

Iranian-Americans can be described as an ethnic group without an Iranian mosque community. Iranian-Americans have not yet built a mosque of their own that offers services entirely in Persian. Most Iranian-American teenagers have received no Islamic teaching. While the typical Iranian-American parent has drifted away from religion, and has lost Islam in the process of gaining personal freedom and material comfort, the second generation Iranian is growing up nonreligious. The fact that the Iranian Shiites in the United States did not publicly support Ayatollah Khomeini's call against Salman Rushdi (the author of Satanic Verses) is an indication of their religious alienation and their growing tolerance. This marginality is currently compounded by the continuing tensions between a secularized America and an anti-secular Iran.

An absence of religious passion among Iranian immigrants in general is not necessarily an over-reaction to the Islamization taking place in Iran. Lack of genuine religious commitment has always been a hallmark of modernized Iranians. My survey of 210 Iranian families in New Jersey shows that only 5 families attend a mosque or participate in weekly religious rituals. It seems that nearly all still declare themselves to be Muslims. Religion has become privatized among modernized Iranians, but it still remains a powerful influence on the Iranian mind in this country, particularly in dealing with the ultimate question of one's existence.

Many of second generation college-age Iranians will live their adult lives in a religious vacuum rather than to be associated with what they regard as the hypocrisy of Institutional religion. Moreover, the preference for empty ceremonialism, usually organized by secular Iranian parents, reinforces the religious alienation of some of the best and most sincere elements of the young generation. Thus, in a country where almost all first and second generation ethnics have their own religious centers, religion has become irrelevant for most second generation Iranians in the United States. In other words, the upbringing and schooling of the Iranian-Americans lack the religious dimension. They find their identity instead in the secularization of the national-cultural aspects of the Iranian tradition.

CHAPTER 12

Communal Life

Rediscovering Persia in America

The Iranian revolution of 1979 put the Iranian community in America on the defensive. In the early 1980's the idea of creating a new Iran was often discussed in the Exile press. The monarchists were called upon to unite as a nation, purchase an island, install the King of Persia, and create a brand new Iran. The fantasy was taken seriously by a segment of the monarchists because they believed that the royal family, through its unestimated wealth, could and should carry on this mission. As time passed and the monarchists proved to be as divided as the other groups in political exile, the idea of a new Iran gave way to the more realistic project of rediscovering Persia here in America.

Among Iranians in America, intellectuals soon became the leading figures in this nationalist movement. To reconstruct a new national identity as Persian in America, they became deeply interested in pre-Islamic Persian civilization. Promotion of Iran's pre-Islamic heritage found ready resonances in the self-identification of Persian in preference to Iranian, especially in light of the hostage crisis in Iran. This revived Persian identity was also based on the assumption that all Americans cherish the Persian cultural heritage.

Thus, a remarkable cultural institution of an essentially pre-Islamic Persian character developed among the Iranian communities. Not suprisingly, the transmission of the ancient mother tongue, Farsi, to the children became the chief indicator of the preservation of the cultural heritage. In the last five years, Iranians, including those that I previously referred to as "Persian Yankees," have founded numerous Farsi schools and traditional art and cultural centers. Perhaps the most common characteristics of these schools is the fact that they are non-religious-oriented institutions. The classes are held on Saturday mornings and the focus is upon Persian language, literature, and culture. As the Farsi press indicates, there are now Farsi schools in every area in which Iranian Americans reside. It seems that the phenomenon of language loyalty found in some other immigrant groups has also prevailed among Iranian-Americans. However, this renewed interest in teaching Farsi to children who live in a cultured milieu that contains no significant elements of their own cultural heritage does not seem to retard the process of Americanization. It may safely be predicted that the second-generation Iranian will soon become structually assimilated within the American society.

Political Orientation

In terms of political orientation, the Iranian community includes both sympathizers with the old regime (monarchists) and post-revolutionary intellectuals, including both Marxist and non-Marxist activists. With the notable exception of Mujahedin-Khalgh, the exile opposition has become less visible in the last few years, with their activities largely limited to publishing newsletters. As the Iranian community in the United States grows or becomes old, Iranian politics loses credibility. Most of the political leaders have become largely discredited figures with no effective organization or significant membership. The political alienation of the exiles was further reinforced when it became a matter of public knowledge that their political organizations have received covert funding from the CIA.

At the present time, the Iranian immigrants in the United States engage in no politics—any politics, Iranian or American. Therefore, in the strictly political sphere, no party divisions similar to those that dominate other ethnic communities have yet evolved in the Iranian community. After years of largely abstaining from organized political activity, Iranian-Americans are beginning to seek a voice in political affairs. However, there is no grass-roots political organization that would embrace all Iranian immigrants. During the last presidential campaign, an ad was placed in community's paper, *Iran Times,* urging Iranians to vote Republican. If Iranians had complied with the political preference normally associated with their income, 50 percent would have voted for George Bush. It comes as no surprise to find Iranian-Americans opposed to Democratic candidates because the Iranian immigrants generally blame the Carter administration for their uprootedness.

Numbers and organization seem to be the key to ethnic politics. As Iranians become increasingly naturalized, they may constitute a political force. In fact, in the next decade, the Iranian community will raise its stature in politics because a significant number of second generation will hold public offices and prominent positions in government.

Devout Iranian Shia

Unlike most of the Iranian immigrants who regard themselves primarily as Iranians and only secondary as Muslims, the devout Iranian Shia is publically and privately a Shiite. In terms of existential identity, religion is stressed, and the cultural and national aspects of "Iranianness" are deemphasized. That is, when it comes to religious observances, his or her religiosity is non-negotiable.

Shiism in the United States seems to be a reaction to both the fierce winds of secularism that have swept the larger Islamic community to the Sunni Conservatism. Devout Iranian Shia today constitute the most integrated immigrant community. Based on my observations, they regularly attend religious services and strictly observe Islamic diet and clothing styles. Although they attend the mosques that are not Iranian in character, they have developed an Iranian Shia community within the Muslim community.

This relatively small Iranian community consists basically of college students, Iranian governmental officials residing temporarily in the United States, businessmen (Bazari) and other permanent students. My survey shows that these families have created their own family Dowreh, in which they maintain a high rate of interdependancy. By isolating themselves socially, these religious families sustain a sense of solidarity and sisterhood/brotherhood relations. Their strict Islamic observations and their support of the Islamic Republic in Iran help to separate them from the larger community. In a sense, being caught between non-Islamic American culture and a highly secularized Iranian community, they create their own marginal culture, a culture in which they attribute their success and happiness to Allah's pleasure in their devotion.

The Islamic centers are the focal points of devout Iranian Muslims. In a society in which political and cultural establishment are extremely secular in operation, the mosque as a territorial identity is sought to provide religious identity for its members. Ten years ago, religious organization in the Iranian community was underdeveloped; today mosques are attended regularly by Iranian families. While so-called nominal Iranian Muslims might not have once visited a mosque, the devout Iranian Muslims look upon the mosque as a means of preserving their religious identity and as a way of eliminating the damaging influences of American culture, especially the appeal of material things for their children. With regard to child socialization, religious families are increasingly providing Islamic teaching programs for their children. In this area, the mosque's role is essential. "The mosque is a safe place for my children to meet others. It is a familiar environment in which my children develop a sense of discipline and identity," said a mother who drives about 60 miles every week to get to the nearest mosque. Thus, a cultural gulf exists between two groups of Iranian children of the same generation in the United States. One seems to develop an Iranian-American Islamic identity. Another develops a self-concept that lacks its major cultural components. Moreover, a gap is also emerging between the religious and non-religious Iranian communities. The religious community remains a culturally integrated part of the Iranian society, even as it struggles to work out the pains of acculturation. The larger secular Iranian community is already acculturated and currently experiencing the dilemmas of dual marginality.

American-Style Islamization

Since the Iranian revolution of 1979, there has been an increasingly intense scholarly interest in Islam, particularly Shia. In the last few years over a hundred books and many more scholarly articles have been published both by Muslim and non-Muslim scholars in the United States. New programs and courses on Islam, with an emphasis on Shia, have also emerged in most of the major American universities. For example, Princeton University has become the first university in the United States with a chair specifically for studies in Shiism. The money ($1.25 million) is provided by an Iranian businessman based in London, who had been an Iranian delegate to the United States in 1950's. Harold Shapiro, the President of Princeton, is reported to have said that "The professorship of Shiite studies not only benefits current scholarship but enriches the training and opportunities for future specialists in this important area (Iran Times, November 18, 1988).

The current interest in Shia also extends to the world of commerce. In addition to the newly founded academic organizations, a Washington based business enterprise called "The Foundation for Traditional Shiites" has recently come up with a remarkable advertising plan. The plan is part of a new film series on Islam which will be broadcast in late 1991 on American public TV and by major TV stations throughout the world. A contribution of $50,000 or more toward the cost of the program ($4 million budget) will guarantee a sponsor's name in the series. The series, entitled *Islam and the West,* is designed to present an in-depth view of the Islamic civilization in interaction with the West. It will illustrate the important role Islam played in the development of Western culture and how the two civilizations were compatible throughout history (Muslim Journal, September 5, 1986).

CHAPTER 13

Anti-Iranian Reaction

The modern American society is created by many ethnic groups and virtually all of them suffered mockery and abuse at one time or another; but few ethnic outgroup relations in the United States have had a more positive beginning than that which characterized the experiences of the Iranian immigrants from 1950 to 1979. Prior to November 4, 1979, when a group of radical Iranian students took over the American Embassy in Tehran, Iran and America were close friends; and America's attitude toward Iranians in America was positive, resulting primarily from the medical and educational services of Iranian immigrants in the United States. Generally, the Iranian immigrant represented a highly select group of educated Iranians predisposed to accept and emulate the American way of life. In addition, from 1950 to 1979, as estimated 800,000 to 850,000 Americans had visited or lived in Iran. Whether as Peace Corp volunteers or scholars and diplomats, Americans returning from Iran had often expressed their admiration for the Iranian people. More recently many of the American diplomats held hostage in Iran publicly praised the Iranian culture and people while condemning those responsible for their captivity.

Informed Americans considered the western-educated Iranians as the "Middle Eastern Yankee" and associated them with an ancient civilization which produced rich literary heritage of poetry and the beauty of the Persian rug. They also identified with Cyrus the Great, who 2500 years ago introduced the first declaration of Human Rights.

As American-trained professionals, the Iranian immigrants had a greater opportunity for social contact with Americans than was available to most immigrant groups. They also frequently married non-Muslim Americans and as a group enjoyed great success and recognition in their community. Every year on the occasion of the Persian New Year (March 21), greetings from numerous cabinet members, senators, congressmen, and mayors appeared in the community's newspaper. In all of these greetings, Iranian-Americans were referred to as "people with a proud heritage" and were admired for their contributions to the enrichment of American society.

During the same period, Iranian people also had a rather positive attitude toward America and Americans. Iranians saw America as a liberating force whose influence would protect Iran from its traditional enemies (Britain and the Soviet Union). In fact, until 1951, pro-Americanism was one of the most striking features of Iranian nationalism. The pioneer Americans who came to to Iran with their impressive medical and educational services captured the heart of the Iranians, not only as dedicated professionals, but also as sympathetic individuals with a sense of solidarity with the Iranian people. For example, Howard Baskervill, an American teacher living in Iran in 1905, took an active part and lost his life in the Iranian Constitutional revolution. He was sometimes referred to as the American Lafayette in Iran.

However, Iranian attitudes toward America changed with a dramatic suddenness after its role in the overthrow of Dr. Muhammad Mussaddign (August 1953) and the restoration of the Shah. United States policy, not the American people, created a strong undercurrent of anti-Americanism among Iranian intellectuals. This anti-Americanism was increasingly intensified by America's close relationship with the Shah, whom the intelligensia considered a despotic client of the United States. Nevertheless, it was actually during the antimonarchical revolutionary movement of the 1978-79, with its sharp anti-American edge, that the anti-Americanism reached its apex as forcibly demonstrated in the hostage-taking of November 4, 1979.

The hostage crisis brought about a new era in Iranian-American relations—an era still dominated by hatred, distrust, violence, and the most adverse consequences for Iranian-Americans. The American mass media turned its complete attention to the event, and as nightly fare brought angry Iranians shouting "Death to America" into the American home. During the entire fourteen months of the crisis, American citizens (including Iranian-Americans) watched in helpless anger and horror as the slogans "Death to America" and "Death to the Liberals" became increasingly intertwined in the ritualistic chants of the religious masses in Tehran. Thus, anti-Iranian sentiments emerged as the first xenophobic reaction to the humiliation of America during the hostage crisis, and the hatred of Iranians grew fast and deep among Americans. A Harris Poll taken in February 1987 showed that a majority of Americans named only one country as an "enemy"—Iran—compared to only 39 percent who regarded the Soviet Union as an enemy. Another poll taken after Americans mistakingly shot down an Iranian passenger plane (in July 1989 with 290 victims) revealed a deep public antipathy that even defied the traditional humane spirit of Americans. Suprisingly enough, 71 percent said that the missile attack on the plane was justified. Nearly two-thirds of the respondents opposed compensation for the victims. The deep public antipathy toward Iranians was also expressed dramatically in a particularly sick example of humor that circulated in Washington the week after the shootdown: The President wired Iran his regrets after the Iran airplane was shot down, saying "we regret there were 10 empty seats on the Airbus." Such an attitude could be interpreted as an American dislike not for the Iranian government but also for the Iranian people. In fact, during this period, President Reagan echoed a widespread anti-Iranian sentiment when he publicly declared Iran to be "barbaric," "uncivilized," and "stupid." In the climate suggested by such statements, usually more tolerant and open-minded Americans found it justifiable to say derogatory things about Iranians.

Consequently, in a manner reminiscent of the experiences of Japanese Americans in the 1940's, Iranians residing in the United States became the immediate targets of American anger and frustration. Paradoxically, Iranian immigrants and the political refugees who allied themselves with Americans against the extremist religious government in Iran felt that Americans resented them and unfairly blamed them for the hostage crisis.

The anti-Iranian reaction was so widespread that it forced many Iranian-Americans to either change their names or to misrepresent their ethnic identity. During the hostage crisis, one's Iranian identity became a stigma to be hidden or evaded as much as possible. To avoid potential confrontations and differential treatment, most Iranian-Americans started to call themselves Persian-Americans. However, as the conflict between Iran and America escalated, more and more anti-Iranian incidents of varying degrees of seriousness occurred within the Iranian-American community. According to newspaper accounts, the incidents included fire bombings of Iranian businesses, physical assaults, the firing of Iranian nationals (for example, the firing of Iranian bus drivers in the South), the posting of such signs as "no dogs and no Iranians allowed," and the expulsion of Iranian students and the doubling of their tuition at one of the colleges of Mississippi. My own research in several Iranian communities indicated that about 70 percent of the Iranian-Americans in each community said they had experienced anti-Iranian reactions during the hostage crisis.

Among Iranian-Americans, the last ten years of hatred toward Iranians loom as a decisive experience which has had a devastating effect upon their children. Negative characterizations have had a terrifying damaging effect on the psyche of Iranians. The psychological damage, done to second generation Iranians, possibly irreversible, was evident when school-aged children began to display feelings of inferiority and insecurity. In two instances witnessed by the author, two school-aged children, complaining of being identified as an "Iranian terrorists" by other children, went as far as asking their parents to buy them green contact lenses to look like non-Iranians. Such feelings of self-hatred and shame among second generation Iranians in America, which continues to be reinforced by negative images and slurs, remains a major concern among many Iranian-American parents.[1]

Despite all hardship of living in a hostile environment, Iranian-Americans did not collectively respond to anti-Iranian sentiments. In a community as hopelessly divided and fragmented as that of the Iranians, each political faction responded in its own way. Pro-monarchists who opposed the Islamic Republic publicly stated that the Iranian government made Iran the Americans' most hated nation. Therefore, they resented the tendancy of many Americans to equate all Iranians with the Islamic republic and its anti-American policies. Other groups felt that Ayatollah Khomeni's anti-Americanism, unlike the Shah's pro-Americanism, gave rise to a conscious sense of being Iranian among Iranian-Americans. Several letters and essays published in the Iran Times have made the following point:

> Whatever you may think of Khomeini you have to admit this fact. He has made Iran an internationally recognized identity. He brought more respect for the Iranian people than anybody else. The Shah gave us an artificial recognition, but Khomeini gave us our own self-respect. (*Iran Times,* July 14, Aug. 21, 1987)

But an assertion of lost national pride was more frequent in the Immigrant Press. However, the dual marginality of the Iranian immigrant included both self-denegration and ultranationalistic self-assertion. The latter sometimes viewed by Iranian-Americans themselves as a defensive psychic overcompensation. (*Iran Times,* September 21, 1987)

The resulting defensiveness among Iranian-Americans gave them a common focus, drawing them together to some extent, and really, providing a foundation for sustaining a sense of Iranian identity and community. Even if Iranians in the U.S. rejected and despised the Iranian state, their common plight as victims of American public opinion provided some sense of commonality, of shared misery, and thus, of community. It is even possible to suggest that their common defensiveness is what elevated their interest in ethnicity (as expressed in the renewed interest in Farsi, for example) to the level of conscious awareness, identifying it as something to be preserved, and therefore, as an object of community-wide interest.

CHAPTER 14

Summary

The Iranian experience in the United States has been a blend of ethnic pride and resourceful participation in American society. In its early years it is the story of highly educated immigrants who have made substantial contributions to American society. They have gained great prominence in such professions as medicine and academia and business. Unlike other immigrants, post-revolutionary Iranian immigrants also brought cash to invest. Thousands of newcomers put their college degrees aside to be rug dealers, car dealers, real estate agents, and store owners. Iranian-Americans have the highest per-capita income of all ethnic groups in America. The immigrants' children, the second generation, are now crowding into the top professional schools—mainly medicine and law. In my sample of 100 college-age Iranian-Americans, 98 percent are attending college. Out of this, 45 percent are in medical school, 25 percent in law, and 15 percent in business school. The second generation reflects the Iranian reverence for higher education, and it studies compulsively like other ethnic children.

Not all Iranians who fled the country were part of an affluent group. Among the educated Iranians were a large number of refugees who were unable to follow their own line of training. For example, the entry of former army officers into the American occupational structure has been marked by downward mobility and some disappointments. These Iranian immigrants are well educated by Iranian standards, but after a lifetime of military service they are now driving cabs or managing their own stationary shops. According to my investigations, most of these displaced Iranians in their new jobs and trades exhibit a work ethic that reduces the exalted Protestant ethic to indolence.

Today in "Little Irans" in America's major metropolitan areas, almost 400,000 Iranians, now permanently settled and well established, are forming their own sense of identity and community. In doing so, they borrow heavily from their host society, also from their experiences in contemporary Iran, and especially from the resurrected imagery, symbolism, and cultural heritage of ancient Persia. In this state, even as the Iranian-American community continues to assimilate to the American context, it rummages the distant past to self-consciously maintain and/or recreate an older ethnic identity.

The Iranian-American community is fairly unique in a sense: it is undergoing assimilation to the American context just like most other imigrant communities have done. At the same time, however, the defensiveness caused by the hostage crisis, and the fact that the Iranians have a very strong literary and cultural heritage, has led them to search the distant past to self-consciously attempt to create an ethnic identity that is grounded more in ancient Persia, since they apparently have some difficulty identifying with contemporary Iran. So, the ethnic identity and community they are creating is not simply Iranian, as modified by the American experience; it is also something else, something broader, as a result of their rejection of contemporary Iran. Ethnic identity and community is being adapted not just to America, but also in response to the political situation in Iran. So they turn for symbolism and imagery to something that is neither American nor strictly Iranian.

APPENDIXES

Methods of Research

The data for this study (1972-1974) were primarily gathered through participant observation and interviews with 105 Iranian professional immigrants in the United States. In carrying on this study I was involved in the most sensitive and untouched aspect of the Iranian community, namely, the self-isolation and disillusionment of Iranian professionals. It is no exaggeration to say that one must be an Iranian sharing the mentality of Iranians to understand what an Iranian in this community feels when he is asked to be interviewed about his situation.[1] No matter how trustworthy (although for Iranians nowadays even brothers no longer are trusted) and no matter how sympathetic one is, the immediate feeling is that the investigator must be an agent either of the CIA or of SAVAK (the Iranian intelligence service).[2]

Data collection, as Arthur Vidich maintains, does not take place in a vacuum. "Perspective and perceptions of social reality are shaped by the social position and interests of both the observed and the observer as they live through a passing present."[3] With regard to the Iranian professionals, we must remember that the social dimensions of the situation in which they are living are not easily accessible to an observer.

Perhaps the first and most conspicuous characteristics of the Iranian's social life in this country are his privacy and his self-isolation. Consequently, when these traits are combined with a high degree of suspicion and distrust, it becomes extremely difficult to make an investigation of this kind.[4]

Thus, it was with such a highly over-sensitive, suspicious, and cynical group that I had to work, and as a researcher use special techniques in carrying out the research.

Since I did not know more than thirty professional Iranian families personally, it seemed that the best way to get acquainted with a larger group was to ask these families to introduce me to their friends and associates. At the same time, in order to avoid suspicion about my identity and motives, in requesting cooperation for an interview I used the stationery of the college in which I was teaching. I was perfectly frank and direct in informing the immigrants why I wanted to interview them, and what my objectives were.

No longer an unidentified interviewer or a "mofattesh," I was accepted as an Iranian professional with an established position as a sociologist in an American college. While this somehow lessened the fear that I was an agent seeking information, it gave the impression to some that I was a non-returnee with a sympathetic feeling. Therefore, I realized that throughout the interview I must make sure that my unavoidable sympathies did not render my results invalid.[5] As an Iranian, I also knew that I must do my best not to show personal and political sympathies, in order to hear what the informant had to say rather than what he thought I wanted to hear.

Another problem at this stage was that I had to convince those who were willing to be interviewed about the use of this study. The prevailing attitude was that since I was an Iranian I was "supposed to know everything" because "everybody knows why Iranians are here."[6] I could not justifiably maintain an attitude of naivete. Therefore, I told them that as an Iranian sociologist I needed to know precisely what are those things that "everybody knows." Moreover, I tried to evoke their national pride and Iranian uniqueness by saying that if we believe we are in many ways different from other immigrants, we need to introduce ourselves to the Americans.[7]

Putting aside these preliminary difficulties, perhaps the most important problem that I had to deal with was whether under such circumstances I could get candid responses to my questions. Would the interviewees give me the statements which are operative in identifying themselves? Or would they "be inclined to hide their significant self-attitudes behind an innocuous and conventional front?"[8]

Here I was faced with the familiar doctrine of "Ketman" or "tagiyyah" (dissimulation), which every investigator of Iranian society has encountered.[9] If it is immoral for a Westerner to put up a false front, for an Iranian Shi'i, according to this doctrine, it is indeed legitimate to do so.

The peculiar custom of "ketman" as an accepted mode of behavior can be traced back to the early centuries of Islam. Its practice as a self-defense mechanism permitted an Iranian Shi'i, in danger because of his religious belief, to pretend that he was a Sunnie, a Christian, or a Jew, whichever best served his need for self-protection. According to this belief, it is not only permissible but also quite legitimate for a Shi'i to conceal his faith. In the course of Iranian socio-political experiences, this belief was reinforced and its application extended beyond religion. Further, it aided an Iranian in adapting himself to oppressive social and political conditions.[10]

I must admit that the phenomenon of *ketman* as an opportunistic measure and self-serving device was the most challenging element in undertaking this research. In order to counteract such possible false representation, whenever I thought the situation might justify its practice I used a special device. By this I mean that I asked my informant to tell what other Iranians might think or do, rather than try to elicit his own thinking or practice. As an insider I was at an advantage in this respect because I knew that it is common and easy for an Iranian to talk of himself in collective terms. Questions in this respect, especially with regard to touchy issues, started this way: "What do other Iranians think or do...? Do you know an Iranian who thinks this way...? Are there any Iranians you know that...? It seems that we Iranians are... What do you think?"

Therefore, through this device, while abstaining from stirring up touchy personal questions, I was able to gain much information concerning areas of self-threat and vulnerability. Needless to say, I was more than an observer. Unlike a Western observer who is only aware of *ketman* as a cultural system, I obviously shared the *ketman* practice. Moreover, I had had enough contacts with Iranians in this country to know their orientations, their role preferences, and their role expectations.[11]

During the last six and a half years of my residence in this country, I came in close contact—through my wife, who is a nurse—with at least thirty Iranian physicians and nurses. In my teaching experience at a state college in New Jersey, I became directly and indirectly acquainted with a few Iranian professors. In the past two and a half years, since the idea for this project came into my mind, I frequently visited these individuals and their families and occasionally participated in their social life.

Moreover, because of the lack of any Iranian club or center, I made other observations of Iranians in their social and professional activities in these ways:

1. Whenever there was a charter flight to Iran, I went to the airport and spent a few hours there.
2. For six months I was a patient of an Iranian dentist and met other Iranian patients.
3. As an official court interpreter in New York City I met various Iranians.
4. Every year I attended Iranian New Years parties and there I observed Iranians in one of their national activities.

Participating in these activities and situations had certain significant advantages, perhaps the most important of which was the opportunity to observe the intimate relationships and community life of the immigrants. I was able, as Vidich suggests, "to secure data within the medium, symbols, and experiential worlds which have meaning to the respondents.[12] The famed Iranian individualism, cynicism, and anti-Americanism found their peculiar modes of expression in most of these situations. Thus I had no difficulty in eliciting frequent statements about their orientation. These various observations were also important because I was able later on to cross-check them against the interviews to find "discrepancies between avowals in one context and facts which [were] allowed to 'slip out' in another."[13]

Moreover, having the advantage of participating in these events gave me the chance to seek out individuals for their unique perspectives.[14] At the same time it facilitated my efforts to establish acquaintance with a larger group of immigrants.

The principal technique of research in this study was a lengthy detailed interview questionnaire, in the Persian language, conducted with 105 of the Iranian permanent immigrants in New York, New Jersey, and Pennsylvania. In every case the relationship was explicitly that of investigator and informant. The interview was formal in the sense that it included certain fixed questions which were posed in a constant form to every informant. The informants were encouraged to go beyond the questions and comment on other aspects of their social situation in this country. While they were commenting and often becoming highly emotional, I did my best not to "go native" and "neither to weep nor to laugh, but to understand."

It must be added that since most of the informants understandably were over-cautious, they asked me in advance not to use tape recording devices or their handwriting.[15] Therefore, in many of the cases I had to write the answers myself. Although the interviewees were assured the strictest secrecy, I had to invite some of them (almost 35 percent) to my residence because they so strongly insisted on protecting their "private lives." This was especially true in the case of those who were married to Americans.

Our interview schedule involved the following topics:

1. Socio-economic background of the participants and their present and past occupations

2. Personal characteristics, such as sex, age, marital status, immigration status, ethnic background, and religious affiliation

3. The informants' orientation toward their compatriots in this country, and their participation in the Iranian community

4. The informants' social and professional participation in the larger American society, and their response toward American culture and Americanization

5. The immigrants' perception of his personal and national status, and their orientation toward remigration.

The majority of these 105 individuals had been in this country for more than five years and all without exception were permanent immigrants according to the immigration law. My problem in obtaining a larger sample was the lack of information concerning Iranian immigrants to the United States. Firm demographic facts are non-existent, for no study of any aspects of non-student immigrants exists. The Immigration and Naturalization Service was contacted through a request for data, but I was informed that the Immigration Service has not yet made a distinctive category for the Iranians in this country. That is, Iranians are listed under the category of "others." I was told that even the Iranian embassy does not keep names and addresses of Iranians who have no student visas.

A random sample was impossible. Consequently, names were gathered through friends and other contacts in places such as hospitals, airports, doctors' offices, universities, and social gatherings. More than 250 Iranians were contacted by telephone calls and letters, and of these 105 were willing to be interviewed. In effect, I had no choice except to employ what Camilleri calls a "convenience sample."[16]

However, there are reasons to believe that the members of this sample do have a reasonable degree of representativeness in the broader population. In terms of social class, since Iranian immigrants mostly come from the middle strata of Iranian society, there is probably no considerable variation in their class characteristics. Moreover, since they are a highly selected group, who mostly fall into the category of professionals and are more or less in the same age group, there is little reason to think that Iranians in other parts of the United States differ significantly from these informants. The immigrants in this sample appear to constitute a proportional representation of geographical areas as well as religious affiliation and ethnic background. But in terms of social class and profession the sample is not, of course, representative of Iranian social classes, for the middle class and professional immigrants are over-represented.

TABLE 5

Iranians Naturalized as U.S. Citizens, 1953-75

Year	Number
1953	93
1958	138
1963	260
1965	295
1968	334
1970	416
1971	501
1972	509
1973	578
1974	562
1975	601
TOTAL	4347

SOURCE: Adapted from the Annual Report of U.S. Immigration and Naturalization Service (1953-75).

TABLE 6

Iranian Permanent Residents in the U.S.A.
by Profession (Major Categories), 1967-69

Professional Categories	Numbers
Technological (natural scientists, engineers)	1357
Medical (physicians, dentists, nurses)	657
Social Scientists and educational fields	276
TOTAL	2290

SOURCE: U.S. Immigration and Naturalization Service, Council on International Education and Cultural Affairs, annual indicator of the immigration into the U.S. of aliens in professional and related occupations, Washington, D.C.

TABLE 7

Major Sources of Newcomers to the United States

1965		1981	
1. Canada	38,327	1. Vietnam	43,483
2. Mexico	37,969	2. Philippines	42,316
3. United Kingdom	27,358	3. Korea	32,320
4. Germany	24,045	4. China	27,651
5. Cuba	19,760	5. India	22,607
6. Colombia	10,885	6. Jamaica	18,970
7. Italy	10,821	7. Dominican Republic	17,245
8. Dominican Republic	9,504	8. United Kingdom	15,485
9. Poland	8,465	9. Cuba	15,054
10. Argentina	6,124	10. Laos	13,970
11. Ireland	5,463	11. Canada	13,609
12. Ecuador	4,392	12. Colombia	11,287
13. China and Taiwan	4,057	13. U.S.S.R.	10,543
14. France	4,039	14. Iran	10,410
15. Haiti	3,609	15. Portugal	8,408

SOURCE: U.S. Immigration and Naturalization Service, Annual Report (Washington, D.C.: U.S. Government Printing Office, 1984) Table 13.

TABLE 8

Patterns of Iranian Immigration to the U.S.

		Percent of New Arrivals/Adjusted Immigrants	
Year of Migration	Percent New Arrivals	Who Resided in Iran Before Coming to the United States	Who Intended to Reside or Resided in California
1972	65.0	96.6	27.2
1973	63.9	96.4	27.3
1974	59.7	91.4	35.0
1975	49.1	88.5	31.2
1976	49.6	88.8	30.1
1977	44.8	93.9	37.8
1978	36.2	93.8	39.1
1979	31.0	97.0	41.4
1980	12.9	97.1	34.4
1981	16.3	79.6	31.6
1982	14.5	83.3	42.4
1983	16.8	84.2	40.6
1984	22.1	79.0	42.5
1985	22.2	75.4	45.8
1986	24.7	71.8	49.3

SOURCE: Mehdi Bozorgmehr & George Sabbagh, "High Status Immigrants: A Statistical Profile of Iranians in the United States." Iranian Studies, 21 Number 3-4, 1988.

TABLE 9

Political Refugees Granted Asylum in the U.S. 1981-1985

Country	Number of applicants	Given asylum	% given asylum	% of total asylees	% of total cases decided
World	72719	17276	24	100	100
Iran	18139	11055	61	64	25
Salvador	18969	515	3	3	26
Nicaragua	13567	1548	11	9	19
Poland	5108	1319	26	8	7
Afghanistan	1181	575	49	3	2
Big Five	56964	15012	26	87	78
All Others	15755	2264	14	13	22
Non-Iranians	54580	6221	11	36	75

SOURCE: Immigration and Naturalization Services (INS) 1985. Statistical Yearbook Washington, D.C.: U.S. Government Printing office.

TABLE 10

Largest Groups (Big Five) of Applicants for Asylum in the U.S.

	1982		1983		1984		1985	
Country	Granted	Denied	Granted	Denied	Granted	Denied	Granted	Denied
Iran	2610	1683	1760	561	5017	3216	1668	1844
Afghan.	303	166	53	47	186	269	33	124
Nicaragua	338	950	94	1346	1018	7274	102	2449
Poland	102	1095	261	900	721	1482	235	312
El Salvador	69	1067	71	2914	328	13045	47	1428

SOURCE: Immigration and Naturalization Service.

TABLE 11

General Characteristics of Foreign-Born Residents of the United States as of 1980 (Percentages)

Characteristics	Iranians	Foreign-Born	Native
Under age 15	11	9	24
Over age 64	3	21	11
College graduates	43	16	16
Professionals	27	12	12
Arrived 1975-80	72	24	—
U.S. citizenship	15	51	100
California residents	40	25	10

SOURCE: U.S. Census of Population: Foreign-Born population, 1984.

TABLE 12

Occupational Characteristics of 231 Iranians in New Jersey, 1989*

Engineers	85
Physicians and dentists	60
College professors	37
Nurses (R.N.)	10
Car dealers	9
Store owners	9
Realtors	8
Restaurant owners	7
Managerial, executive	6

* These Iranians are permanent residents and have lived in the United States for more than 10 years.

NOTES

CHAPTER 1

1. Introduction to Stonequist, *The Marginal Man*, p. xvii.
2. Park, "Human Migration and Marginal Man," p. 881.
3. Ibid, p. 893.
4. For an original and insightful critical analysis of Park's "Race-Relation Cycle," see Stanford M. Lyman, *The Black American in Sociological Thought*.
5. Park and Ernest W. Burgess, *Introduction to the Science of Sociology*, pp. 317-22.
6. Stonequist, p. 8.
7. Ibid., pp. 2-3.
8. Ibid., pp. 65-66.
9. Ibid., pp. 66-67.
10. Everett Stonequist, "The Problem of the Marginal Man," p. 11. This article is the basis of discussion in his book *The Marginal Man*.
11. Milton M. Goldberg, "A Qualification of the Marginal Man Theory," pp. 52-58.
12. Ibid., p. 55.
13. Ibid., p. 58.
14. For a major statement on marginal culture as a subculture, see Noel Gist and Anthony Gray Dwokin, *The Blending of Races*, p. 10.
15. Arnold W. Green, "A Re-Examination of the Marginal Man Concept."
16. Ibid., p. 171.
17. H. F. Dickie-Clark, *The Marginal Situation*.
18. Ibid., p. 190.
19. Ibid., p. 195.
20. Ibid., p. 186.
21. Georg Simmel, *The Sociology of Georg Simmel*, pp. 402-8.
22. Ibid., p. 403.
23. For a recent critique of the sociology of the stranger, see S. Dale McLemore, "Simmel's 'Stranger,'" pp. 86-94.
24. Alfred Schutz, "The Stranger," pp. 499-507, and "The Homecomer," p. 999.
25. Ibid., p. 502.
26. Ibid., p. 506.
27. Ibid., p. 502.
28. Schutz, "The Homecomer," p. 309.
29. Ibid., p. 372.
30. For a major statement on analytical (and often empirical) differences of adjustment, integration, and marginality, see Gino Germani (ed.), *Modernization, Urbanization, and the Urban Crisis*.
31. Paul C. P. Siu, "The Sojourner," pp. 34-43.
32. Ibid., p. 34.
33. Ibid.
34. Ibid., p. 35.
35. Ibid.

36. Ibid., p. 36.
37. Ibid., p. 37.
38. Ibid., p. 35.
39. Ibid., p. 43.
40. David Riesman, "Some Observations Concerning Marginality," p. 3.
41. Jawaharlal Nehru, *Toward Freedom*, p. 353.
42. Bahman, Niromand, *Iran*, p. 171.
43. For a recent discussion of marginality in a new context, see Germani, pp. 42-47.

CHAPTER 2

1. "Iran" and "Persia," which are used by foreigners to designate the same country, are not true synonyms. Persians call their country Iran and themselves Irani. In 1935 the Iranian government requested all foreign countries to use the official name "Iran." Thus in this study we tend to use "Iran" when it is applied to modern Persia.
2. Firuz Kazemzadeh, "Ideological Crisis in Iran," p. 196.
3. Alessandro Bausani, *The Persians*, p. 139.
4. With regard to the assimilating tendencies of Persians as early as the Achaemenian Empire (550-331 B.C.), Herodotus reports: "There is no nation which so readily adopts foreign customs as the Persians. As soon as they hear of any luxury they instantly make it their own." Cited in Donald N. Wilber, *Iran Past and Present*, p. 22.
5. For an account of the chronology of the impact of the Western powers upon Iran, see Joseph Upton, *The History of Modern Iran*.
6. Nikki Keddie, "The Iranian Power Structure and Social Chance 1800-1969, p. 6.
7. Hafez Farman Farmayan, "The Forces of Modernization in Nineteenth-Century Iran," p. 120.
8. Ibid., p. 121.
9. For a detailed description of these newspapers, see Farman Farmayan, pp. 146-48.
10. "Pahlavi" is the ancient word for the Persian language, used in the Sassanid Empire (226-651 A.D.).
11. Source: Ministry of Labor, "Barresy-i-niru-i-Ensani..." vol. 3, Tehran, 1964, pp. 2010-43.
12. These individuals are identified as *motajadedin* (innovators).
13. This statement is attributed to Taghizadeh, the leading constitutionalist.
14. The uncritical acceptance of Western intellectual works is still prevalent among contemporary Westernized intellectuals. For instance, it is interesting to note that the book *Toward the Year 2,000*, edited by D. Bell (1970), was translated into Farsi two years after its publication.
15. The first manifestation of hostility of the Iranian toward *khareji* (foreigners) was the movement against the British tobacco monopoly in 1891-92. For a comprehensive study of this movement see Nikki Keddie, *Religion and Rebellion in Iran*.
16. Bahman Niromand, *Iran: New Imperialism in Action*, pp. 37-38. For a detailed description of American involvement in this period see Arthur Millspaugh, *Americans in Persia*.
17. It must be noted, however, that United States involvement in Iranian affairs, beginning in the Cold War era, was not accidental policy. It was indeed an integral part of the general policy of the United States. For a discussion on this point see Joseph Bensman and Arthur Vidich, "The Struggle for the Underdeveloped World."
18. For a comprehensive study of this movement see Richard Cottam, *Nationalism in Iran*.
19. Daniel Lerner, *The Passing of Traditional Society*, p. 38.

20. For example, see Norman Jacobs, *The Sociology of Development,* pp. 24884; James Bill "The Plasticity of Informal Politics," pp. 131-50; and Marvin Zonis, *The Political Elite of Iran,* pp. 199-298. For a merely impressionistic observation of these traits, one can look at almost every travelers' book on Persia.
21. The geographical situation of Iran undoubtedly has had some impact upon Iranian experiences. Internally, Iran is a vast territory with villages that for a long time remained isolated and blocked from communication. Moreover, it has had a distinctive irrigation system (qanat, or kariz), which has been a decisive factor in determination of villagers' rights. Externally, it has a strategic location, which made it an arena of imperial struggle. For a discussion of what is called "hydraulic civilization" see K. Wittfogel, *Oriental Despotism.* For a criticism of this perspective see W. Eberhard, *Conquerors and Rulers.* For another major statement, opposed to Wittfogel's thesis, see B. Barrington Moore, Jr., *Social Origins of Dictatorship and Democracy,* pp. 159-291.
22. Stanford M. Lyman and Marvin B. Scott, *A Sociology of the Absurd,* pp. 8687. The term "sociology of the absurd" is today associated with Lyman and Scott. This perspective emphasizes the essential meaninglessness of the world, and attempts to explain how man makes sense out of his senseless condition. The sociology of the absurd argues that "if life consists of encounters, episodes, and engagements among persons pursuing goals of which they are consciously aware, or about which they can be made aware, then it appears that the fundamental structure of human action is conflict" (p. 5). Thus it assumes "a model of man in conflict-with others, with society, with nature, and even with himself."
23. Quoted in Martin Esslin, *The Theater of the Absurd,* p. xxi. It is interesting that Iranian intellectuals in the past three decades have become increasingly influenced by members of the theater and literature of the absurd, such as Beckett, Ionesco, Camus, Sartre, and Kafka. Kafka's "Metamorphosis" was among the first books translated into Farsi. The influence of literature of the absurd is seen among many Iranian writers and poets, such as Sadegh Hedayat and more recently Nader-i-Ebrahimi.
24. William Haas, *Iran,* p. 119.
25. Ibid., p. 129.
26. For a discussion of the doctrine of *ketman* as an obstacle in undertaking this study, see Appendix 1.
27. Both Frye and Zonis report that the practice of ketman is prevalent in contemporary Iranian society. See Richard N. Frye, *The United States and Turkey and Iran,* p. 208, and Zonis, pp. 199-298.
28. Cited in A. Reza Arasteh, *Man and Society in Iran,* p. 44.
29. Ibid.
30. For a major statement on this point sec Lyman and Scott, p. 19.
31. In my own personal experience as a land reform officer, during 1966-68, in Iranian villages, there were occasions when the landlord was present at a meeting. The villagers would not even acknowledge their cultivators' rights in his presence.
32. Erving Goffman, *The Presentation of Self in Everyday Life,* p. 62.
33. Lerner, p. 357.
34. Jacobs, p. 250.
35. Ibid., p. 13.
36. Much contemporary Iranian literature, particularly what is called new wave poetry, contains such themes as deception, walls, locks, nothingness, helplessness, and meaninglessness.
37. For the most comprehensive analysis of contemporary Iranian social structure, see James A. Bill, *The Politics of Iran.*
38. During the past two decades Western social scientists have been inquiring for a

new middle class in the Middle Eastern countries that could assume primary responsibility for all phases of development. See M. Halpern, *The Politics of Social Change in the Middle East,* and A. Perlmutter, *"The Myth of the New Middle Class."*
39. Source: *UN Statistical Yearbook,* 1953, p. 528, and *Kayhan International,* Tehran, June 28,1974.
40. Hossein G. Askari and John Thomas Cummings, *The Middle East and the United States: A Problem of "Brain Drain,"* p. 79.
41. Bill, *The Politics of Iran,* p. 53.
42. The term "Western-struck" was first coined by Jalal Al-i Ahmad, an Iranian intellectual who for the first time in the early 1960s warned the Iranian elites against uncritical acceptance of Western products.
43. Karl Mannheim, *Essays on the Sociology of Culture,* p. 144.
44. There are many unsettled questions about the basis and characteristics of classes in Iranian society, just as there are about strata and status groups. In spite of these conceptual problems, there are some general features about status groups which are empirically valid.
45. For an earliest exposition of the phenomenon of status community, see Thorstein Veblen, *The Theory of the Leisure Class.*
46. This refers to those individuals who enter the middle class but do not carry along their own immediate social unit. For instance, a university professor or an outstanding doctor may have uneducated parents living in a small town or rural area.
47. Bill, *The Politics of Iran,* pp. 70-72.

CHAPTER 3

1. It seems that the whole cultural setting and the Iranian consciousness of rich cultural heritage weigh against permanent migration. In Iranian literature one who leaves home and friends (tark-i yar va diar) has no honored place among his people.
2. U.S. Immigration and Naturalization Service.
3. Gregory Henderson, "Foreign Students: Exchange or Immigration," p. 20.
4. Hosein Ali Ronaghi, "Mohajerat-i-Pezeshgan" (migration of physicians).
5. Kayhan International, June 20, 1973.
6. For a historical background of such conflict of interest, see Manfred Halpern, *The Politics of Social Change in the Middle East and North Africa,* pp. 51-78.
7. Daniel Lerner, *The Passing of Traditional Society,* p. 369.
8. By legitimacy of the political system we mean the capacity of the political authority to engender and maintain the belief that the existing political institutions are the most appropriate ones for the society. Max Weber recognized three principles- "charismatic," "traditional," and "legal" which permit this legitimate exercise of the power to issue commands. For a discussion of legitimacy based on charismatic leadership and traditional authority, see Max Weber, *Economy and Society,* pp. 941-54.
9. The only existing study of repatriated Iranians reveals that "three-fourths of the sample (N-414) reported that at some point in their foreign experience they had seriously considered emigration and pursuing a foreign career." Moreover, the same study shows that "despite the strength of patriotism in bringing people back, about half the respondents reported 'close friends' who had chosen foreign careers." In terms of alienation and disillusionment among the returnees, it reveals that "significantly, over 60 percent of the sample (256) reported that they had friends who have returned to Iran but now wish they had not. Three-quarters of these thought that more than half their returned friends regretted having come back; only a quarter limited this assessment to a 'very few of their friends.'" See George B. Baldwin, "The Foreign-Educated Iranian: A Profile," pp. 267-68. The UNESCO study of Ira-

nian, Egyptian, and Indian returnees also reveals that only 9 percent of the Iranian returnees were "happy to be home again." Cited in James Bill, "The Politics of Student Alienation," pp. 8-26. It must be added that none of these studies has determined to what extent the resulting frustration has had political roots.
10. The social and cultural alienation the returned Iranian experiences is well expressed in several literary works by Iranian foreign-educated writers such as Jamalzadeh, Hedayat, and Esfandiary, In English, see F. M. Esfandiary, *Identity Card*. For an analysis of elite Iranians attitudes toward friends and family, see Marvin Zonis, *The Political Elite of Iran*, pp. 277, 283.
11. In talking of developing countries in general, it is of course difficult to make a clear-cut distinction between professional structures and political factors. In Iranian society they seem to be closely interconnected. However, for the sake of clarification an attempt will be made to identify those elements which are related to professional structures.
12. For an excellent analysis of frustration of a group of American-trained returnees resulting from what James Bill calls "the pattern of polarities of the Iranian web system," see James Bill, "The Iranian Intelligentsia: Class and Change," Ph.D. dissertation, Princeton University, 1968, pp. 184-205.
13. Lerner, p. 368.
14. James Bill, "Iranian Intelligentsia," p. 165.
15. Ibid.

CHAPTER 4

1. Harold Margulies and Lucille Stephenson Bloch, *Foreign Medical Graduates in the United States*, p. 80.
2. This finding is consistent with Margulies and Bloch, p. 21.
3. Fifty percent of the Iranian population in 1964 were less than twenty years of age, and 30 percent were between the ages of fifteen and thirty. Source: Ministry of Labor, Tehran, 1964.
5. George B. Baldwin, "The Foreign-Educated Iranian," p. 272.
6. According to immigration law, individuals with J visas may request a waiver of the requirement that they go home for at least two years. For a discussion of immigration policies concerning medical graduates in the United States, see Margulies and Bloch.
7. The Mutual Educational and Cultural Exchange Act (Public Law 87-256), enacted on September 21, 1961, stipulates that the attorney general "may waive the requirement of the two year foreign residency abroad in the case of any alien whose admission to the United States is found by the Attorney General to be in the public interest." Margulies and Bloch found that some of the Persian physicians changed their status through this process. Permanent visa does not preclude the individual's ultimate return to his country; neither does it necessarily mean that he will become a naturalized United States citizen. Furthermore, according to immigration requirements, a permanent resident doctor is permitted to practice medicine without being a citizen.
8. It is possible that the respondents practiced "ketman" and did not reveal their status as citizens of the United States. The main reason behind this concealment is the fact that the Iranian government does not recognize dual citizenship.
9. Mohammad Borhanmanesh, "A Study of Iranian Students in Southern California," p. 82.
10. See Iraj Valipour, "A Comparison of Returning and Non-Returning Iranian Students in the United States," Ed.D. dissertation, Columbia University, 1961.

11. Salo Wittmayer Baron, *A Social and Religious History of the Jews,* p. 125-26.
12. This classification is more or less arbitrary, and the types are usually not refined. I find these types heuristically useful for understanding the meaning each person gives for his or her marginal position.
13. The term "Persian Yankee" is borrowed from an autobiographical book entitled *Ali, A Persian Yankee,* by Maxine A. Miller, as told by Ali Azizi (a former Iranian student in the United States).
14. This kind of unfavorable attitude toward the Iranian emigrant has to do with the fact that Iranians historically have not accepted emigration as a mode of action. This orientation is furthermore reinforced by the fact that the Iranian emigrant is, paradoxically, a student who has failed to fulfill his original cause or "mission," namely, obtaining education and returning home. The 105s of such an individual for both the family and the nation is regarded a real tragedy. This unfavorable attitude toward Iranians abroad was expressed by some cabinet members during a "brain drain" debate in 1973.
15. Borhanmanesh, "A Study of Iranian Students," and Valipour, "A Comparison."
16. David Riesman, "Some Observations Concerning Marginality," p. 3.
17. For a description of the radical intellectual as a permanent alien, see Plato, *Republic* (Cornford transl.), bk. 6, ch. 22.
18. James Bill, "The Iranian Intelligentsia," p. 195.
19. Letter to the editor, *Iran Times* (December 8, 1972), p. 3, no. 1.
20. Ibid., December 15, 1972, p. 5, no. 2.

CHAPTER 5

1. The term "chain migration" implies "the processes by which newcomers learned of opportunities, were provided with passage money, and had initial accommodation and employment arranged through previous immigrants." See John S. MacDonald and L. D. MacDonald, "Urbanization, Ethnic Group and Social Segregation," p. 435.
2. Don Martindale, *American Social Structure,* pp. 386-95.
3. E. Stonequist, *The Marginal Man,* p. 85.
4. See Judith Kramer, *American Minority Community,* p. 213.
5. For an analytical discussion of the concept of "Territoriality," see Lyman and Scott, *Social Problems* 12 (no. 4,1967), pp. 236-49.
6. Judith Kramer, pp. 125-34.
7. Maurice R. Stein, *The Eclipse of Community,* p. 276.
8. Apparently, the favorable market situation has been changing. Sentiment against alien professionals is already on the way to actualization. For an emerging new nativism against alien professionals, see Leslie Aldridge Westoff, "Should We Pull Up the Gangplank?"
9. For a discussion of the terms "the community" and "community," see Jessie Bernard (ed.), *The Sociology of Community,* p. 3.
10. Kramer, p. 85.
11. As reported in my postscript, this aspect has significantly changed since 1977.
12. *Directory of Iranian Students Association in the United States* (New York: Iranian Students Association, n.d.), p. i.
13. As of 1977.
14. Since 1979 the *Iran Times* has reached much larger numbers of the Iranian community and has become the most popular Iranian newspaper in the United States.

CHAPTER 6

1. Max Weber, *Economy and Society,* pp. 4042.
2. See Max Weber, "Ethnic Groups," 1, pp. 385-98.
3. Stein, p. 112.
4. Stanford M. Lyman, *The Asian in the West,* p. 57.
5. Robert Nisbet, *Community and Power,* p. 230.
6. In the case of Jews, see, for example, K. Lewin, *Resolving Social Conflicts.* For Italians, sec Irvin I. Child, *Italian or Americans* and Joseph Lopreato, *Italian Americans*

CHAPTER 7

1. Everett Stonequist, *The Marginal Man,* p. 88.
2. Once mixed marriages occur, the pattern seems to be a reluctant acceptance of of the act by the parents. See Anne Sinclair Mehdevi, *Persian Adventures.*
3. Robert E, Park, "Immigrant Community and Immigrant Press," 3, p. 144.
4. It is interesting to note that while the immigrant consciously rejects Americanization, he makes no attempt to transfer his culture to his children. The majority of the immigrants' children do not speak Farsi. In terms of their lack of knowledge of their fathers' culture, the children as the second generation resemble more that of third generation immigrants in this country. See Chapter 9 on Immigrants and Their Children.

CHAPTER 8

1. In Iran titles such as "doctor," "professor," and "engineer" are most important in the framework of individual social relationships. Degrees and titles are normally used to address a person at work and on the street. An engineer is addressed as "Engineer So and So." The wife of a physician is called "Doctor's Wife."
2. For an analytical discussion of "excuse" and "justification" as types of "account," see Stanford M. Lyman and Marvin B. Scott, pp. 111-43.
3. Everett Hughes, "Dilemmas and Contradictions of Status," *American Journal of Sociology* 5, pp. 353-59.

CHAPTER 9

1. The second generation in my sample (in 1977) was only at preschool and school age. I interviewed thirty couples who were in New York and New Jersey areas. The Iranian parents in this sample consists of twenty Iranian and ten Iranian-American couples. They are all highly educated professionals. Almost all the wives have college degrees. While the children were only observed, the parents were questioned in detail about their attitudes toward the ethnic identity of their children.
2. For a discussion of the traditional Iranian family and its persisting characteristics, see A. Ansari, "The Traditional Iranian Family and Modernizing Influences," in *Sociological Perspectives in Marriage and the Family,* ed. Mildred W. Weil pp. 334-48.
3. Milton Gordon, *Assimilation in American Life,* p. 234.
4. From a somewhat different perspective, these orientations appear to be stages along a continuum of the assimilation process.

CHAPTER 10

1. As reported in the *New York Times*, Immigration and Naturalization Service, *May 26, 1985.*
2. "The New Ellis Island," *Time*, June 13,1983, pp. 117.
3. Ibid,, p. 13. In this article it is reported that "some American parents worry that their children's education is suffering as teachers slow their lessons to accommodate the Farsi speakers." But one Iranian mother reports: "When we bought their houses and raised the price from $1 million to $3 million, they were not complaining."
4. In a letter to the editor of *The Iran Times*, an Iranian immigrant admits that he has become a citizen of the United States and encourages others to do the same thing. *Iran Times*, July 22,1983.

PART III INTRODUCTION

*The field work on which this study is based was carried out during 1985-1989. The data was primarily gathered through participation and interviews with over 400 Iranians in Los Angeles, Seattle, Washington, D.C., New York and New Jersey. As a director of Persian language program, I have also observed over 30 second generation teenage Iranians every Saturday for two hours, the last three years. This essay extends my discussion of "Iranians in America: Continuity and Change" to be published in Vincent Parrillo's *Rethinking Today's Minorities*, Greenwood Press. 1991.

CHAPTER 13

1. Another area in which native-born Americans were able to express openly their hostility toward the Iranians was in the Wrestling circuit. Since the early 1980's an Iranian immigrant known as the Iron Sheik, has regularly performed as a "bad guy" on the American wrestling circuit. By capitalizing on his Iranian nationality, he created an outlet for Americans' frustration over Iran. American wrestling fans have always enjoyed loosing the Iron Sheik and taking out their anger over Iranian-American political conflict.

APPENDIXES

1. Refers to the period (1974 to 1977) that the data was collected.
2. It is commonly believed by almost every Iranian intellectual that most of the books on Iran are written either by travelers or by social scientists who have been part of the grand artifice of some externally stimulated master plan of "imperialist powers." As a result of this belief, some Iranian students in this country who read these books in the library do not hesitate to cross out those paragraphs with which they disagree or to notify other readers of the writers' State Department ties.
3. Vidich, "Participant Observation and the Collection and Interpretation of Data," p. 360.
4. There are of course understandably political reasons for such widespread suspicion and distrust. But the unwillingness of Iranians to be questioned or observed lies also in their cultural traits. The typical Iranian has no regard for a researcher. His conception of a researcher is that of *mofattesh* or *fuzul* (inspector or meddler). A *mofattesh* is indeed a government agent whose intention is to use his collected information against the individual's interest. A *fuzul* is a person, not necessarily an

agent, who by asking private and personal questions is also thought to violate the respondent's private life. Thus, in presenting himself to the observer, the Iranian either rejects the invitation or if he accepts will try to hide behind a psychological wall and maintain a false front. It is interesting to note that even high walls around the house, which were traditionally made to protect the Iranian and his family from outsiders, have not provided a sense of security for the Iranian. "Walls have mice, and mice have ears" is a Persian saying. Such belief also dominates the mind of Iranians in this study.

5. As Howard S. Becker rightly points out, we can never avoid taking sides. For a major statement on this point, see "Whose Side Are We On?" pp. 23943.

6. The common attitude i5 that "everybody knows the problem." This attitude is especially prevalent in the case of politically minded professionals and self-proclaimed Marxists. For instance, among the professionals, physicians usually claim a vast knowledge in almost every field. It is indeed "improper" for them to confess their ignorance of anything. After all Iranians used to call Physician by the Arab word *hakim* (philosopher). To the Iranian Marxist the Iranian situation seems clear because he gives an over-simplified interpretation of "general laws of development."

7. I explained to some of my informants that I might later expand this study into a book about Iranians in the United States.

8. Manford H. Kuhn and Thomas S. MacPartland, "An Empirical Investigation of Self-Attitudes," p. 168.

9. For example, see Daniel Lerner, *The Passing of Traditional Society*, p. 358, and his review in *American Sociological Review* 19 (1954), p. 488. See also Czeslaw Milosz, *The Captive Mind*.

10. Both Frye and Zonis maintain that the practice of *ketman* is a prevalent behavior in contemporary Iranian society. See Richard N. Frye, *The United States and Turkey and Iran*, p. 208, and Marvin Zonis, *The Political Elites of Iran*, pp. 199-298.

11. The following example indicates how I was able to note and check the practice of *ketman*. I asked my informant if he taught his children the Iranian language. The answer usually was in the affirmative. As I knew that he might be practicing *ketman*, I arranged later to meet the children at home and found that they did not in most cases know even a few Iranian words.

12. Vidich, p. 554.

13. Vidich and Gilbert Shapiro, "A Comparison of Participant Observation and Survey Data," p. 28.

14. For a major statement of this point, see Howard S. Becker, "Interviewing Medical Students," p. 201.

15. It is interesting to note that in some cases the informant introduced himself by his first name and was reluctant to mention his last name. This is of course a common attitude among Iranians in this country, especially among students, who might know many compatriots by their first names.

16. Santo F. Camilleri, "Theory, Probability, and Induction in Social Research," p. 174.

REFERENCES

BOOKS

Al-i Ahmad, Jalal. Charbzadegi (Western-Struck), Tehran, 1962.
Arasteh, Reza. *Man and Society in Iran.* Leiden: E. J. Brill, 1970.
Banani, Amin. *The Modernization of Iran, 1921-1941.* Stanford: Stanford University Press, 1961.
Baron, Salo Wittmayer. *A Social and Religious History of the Jews.* New York: Columbia University Press, 1937.
Bausani, Alessandro. *The Persians.* London: Elek Books Ltd, 1971.
Bell, Daniel, ed. *Toward the Year 2000.* Boston: Houghton Mifflin, 1968.
Bendix, Reinhard. *Embattled Reason.* New York: Oxford University Press, 1970.
Bendix, R., and Martin Lipset. *Social Mobility in Industrial Society.* Berkeley: University of California Press, 1959.
Bernard, Jessie, ed. *The Sociology of Community.* Glenview, III.: Scott, Foresman, 1973.
Bill, James A. *The Politics of Iran: Groups and Classes and Modernization.* Columbus: Charles E. Merriu, 1972.
Bozorgmehr, M. and G. Sabagh. 1988. "High Status Immigrants: A Statistical Profile of Iranians in the United States." *Iranian Studies.* (pp. 5-13)
Child, Irvin L., *Italian or American?* New Haven: Yale University Press, 1943.
Cottam, Richard W. *Nationalism in Iran.* Pittsburgh: University of Pittsburgh Press, 1964.
Dickie-Clark, H. F. *The Marginal Situation.* London: Routledge & Kegal Paul, 1967.
Eberhard, W. *Conquerors and Rulers.* Berkeley: University of California Press, 1967.
Esfandiary, F. *Identity Card.* New York: Grove Press, 1966.
Esslin, Martin. *The Theater of the Absurd.* Garden City: Doubleday Anchor, 1961.
Farman Farmayan, Hafez. "The Forces of Modernization in Nineteenth-Century Iran." *Beginnings of Modernization in the Middle East,* ed. William R. Polk and Richard Chambers. Chicago: University of Chicago Press, 1968.
Frye, Richard N. *Persia.* New York: Shocken Books, 1960.
---. *The United States and Turkey and Iran.* Cambridge: Harvard University Press, 1951.
Germani, Gino, ed. *Modernization, Urbanization and the Urban Crisis.* Boston: Little, Brown, 1973.
Gerschenkron, Alexander. *Economic Backwardness in Historical Perspectives.* New York: Praeger, 1965.
Gist, NoeL and Anthony G. Dworkin. *The Blending of Races: Marginality and Identity in World Perspective.* New York: John Wiley and Sons, 1972.
Glazer, Nathan and Daniel Moynihan. *Beyond the Melting Pot.* Boston: M.I.T. Press, 1970.
Goffman, Erving. *The Presentation of Self in Everyday Life.* New York: Doubleday, 1959.
Gordon, Milton M. *Assimilation in American Life.* New York: Oxford University Press, 1964.

Haddad, 1987. *Islamic Values in the U.S.* New York: Oxford University Press, Inc. (p. 51)

Halpem, Manfred. *The Politics of Social Change in the Middle East and North Africa.* Princeton: Princeton University Press, 1963.

Hass, William S. *Iran.* New York: Columbia University Press, 1946.

Iqbal, Mohammad. *Seyre-i phalsafeh dar Iran* (The Development of ethaphysics in Iran). In Farsi. Tehran: Regional Cultural Institute, 1968.

Jacobs, Norman. *The Sociology of Development: Iran as an Asian Case Study.* New York: Pragger, 1966.

Jamalzadeh, Mbhammad. *Yeki Bud, Yeki Naboud* (Once upon a Time). Tehran: Amirkabir, 1938/1959.

Kazemzadeh, Firuz. "Ideological Crisis in Iran" *The Middle East in Transition,* ed Walter Laqueur. New York: Praeger, 1956.

Keddie, Nikki. *Religion and Rebellion in Iran: The Tobacco Protest of 1891-1842.* London: Frank Cass, 1966.

Kramer, Judith. *American Minority Community.* New York: Thomas Y. Crowell, 1970.

Kuhn, Manford H., and Thomas S. McPartland. "An Empirical Investigation of Self-Attitudes," *Sociological Methods,* ed. Norman Denzin. Chicago: Aldine-Atherton, 1970.

Lerner, Daniel. *The Passing of Traditional Society: Modernizing the Middle East.* New York: The Free Press, 1958.

Lewin, K. *Resolving Social Conflict.* New York: Harper and Row, 1948.

Lopreato, Joseph. *Italian Americans.* New York: Random House, 1970.

Lyman, Stanford M. *The Asian in the West.* Social Science and Humanities Publication No. 4. Reno: Western Studies Center, Desert Research Institute, University of Nevada System, 1970.

---. *The Black American in Sociological Thought: A Failure of Perspective.* New York: Capricorn Books, 1973.

---. and Marvin B. Scott. *A Sociology of the Absurd.* New York: Appleton-Century Crofts, 1960.

Mannheim, Karl. *Essays on the Sociology of Culture.* London: Routledge, 1956.

Margulies, Harold, and Lucille Stephenson. *Foreign Medical Graduates in the U.S.A.* Cambridge: Harvard University Press, 1969.

Martindale, D. *American Social Structure.* New York: Appleton-Century-Crofts, 1960.

Mehdevi, Anne Sinclair. *Persian Adventures.* New York: Alfred A. Knopf, 1953.

Miller, Maxine A. *Ali, A Persian Yankee.* Caldwell, Idaho: Caxton Printers, 1965.

Millspaugh, Arthur. *Americans in Persia.* Washington, D.C.: Brookings Institute, 1946.

Milosz, Czeslaw. *The Captive Mind,* transl. Jane Zielonko. New York: Vintage Books, 1955.

Minorsky, Vladimir. "Iran: Opposition, Martyrdom, and Revolt in *Unity and Variety in Muslim Civilization,* ed. Gustav von Grunebaum. Chicago: Chicago University Press, 1955.

Montesquieu. *The Persian Letters,* trans. R Loey, New York: World, 1961.

Moore, Jr., Barrington. *Social Origins of Dictatorship and Democracy.* Boston: Beacon Press, 1967.

Nehru, Jawaharlal. *Toward Freedom: The Autobiography of J. Nehru.* New York: John Day, 1942.

Niromand, Bahman. *Iran: The New Imperialism in Achon.* New York: Monthly Review Press, 1969.

Nisbet, Robert. *Community and Power.* New York: Oxford University Press, 1953.

Park, Robert E., and E. Burgess. *Introduction to the Science of Sociology.* Chicago: University of Chicago Press, 1921.
Simmel, Georg. *The Sociology of Georg Simmel,* trans. K. Wolff. Glencoc, 111: The Free Press, 1950.
Stein, Maurice R. *The Eclipse of Community.* Princeton: Princeton University Press, 1960.
Stonequist, Everett U., *The Marginal Man.* New York: Scribner, 1937.
Tiryakian, Edward. "Sociological Perspectives on the Stranger." *The Rediscovery of Ethnicity,* ed. Sallie TeSelle. New York: Harper and Row, 1975.
Upton, Joseph. *The History of Modern Iran: An Interpretation.* Cambridge: Harvard University Press, 1960.
Veblen, Thorstein, *The Theory of the Leisure Class.* New York: Random House, 1966.
Warner, L., and L. Srole. *The Social Systems of American Ethnic Groups.* New Haven: Yale University Press, 1962.
Weber, Max. *Economy and Society.* New York: Bedminster Press, 1968.
Wilber, Donald N. *Iran, Past and Present.* Princeton: Princeton University Press, 1958.
Wittfogel, K. *Oriental Despotism.* New Haven: Yale University Press, 1957.
Yarshater, E. *Iran Faces the Seventies.* New York: Paeger, 1971.
Zabih, S. *The Communist Movement in Iran.* Berkeley: University of California Press, 1966.
Zonis, Marvin. *The Political Elite of Iran.* Princeton: Princeton University Press, 1971.

ARTICLES AND PERIODICALS

Ansari, Abdolmaboud, "The Traditional Iranian Family and Modernizing Influences," in *Sociological Perspectives in Marriage and the Family,* ed. Mildred W. Weil. Danville, Illinois: The Interstate, 1977.
Askari, Hossein and John T. Cummings. "The Middle East and the United States: A Problem of 'Brain Drain,'" *International Journal of Middle East Studies* 8 (1977).
Becker, Howard S. "Interviewing Medical Students." *American Journal of Sociology* (September 1956).
Bensman, Joseph, and Arthur Vidich. "The Struggle for the Underdeveloped World." *Caribbean Review* (Winter 1970).
Becker, Howard. "Whose Side Are We On" *Social Problems* 14 (1966).
Bill, James. "The Politics of Student Alienation: The Case of Iran." *Iranian Studies* 2 (winter 1969).
---. "The Plasticity of Informal Politics: The Case of Iran." *Middle East Journal,* (Spring, 1973).
Baldwin, George. "The Foreign-Educated Iranian: A Profile." *Middle East Journal* 17 (summer 1983).
Camilleri, Santo F. "Theory, Probability, and Inaction in Social Research." *American Sociological Review* 6 (February 1941).
Green, Arnold. "A Re-Examination of the Marginal Man Concept." *Social Forces* 26 (December 1947).
Halpem, M. "The New Middle Class in Middle Eastern Countries." *Comparative Studies in Sociology and History* 12 (1970).
Henderson, Gregory, "Foreign Students: Exchange Immigration." *International Development Review* (December 1964).
Hughes, Everett. "Social Change and Status Protest." *Phylon,* first quarter (1949).

---. "Dilemmas and Contradictions of Status." *American Journal of Sociology* 5 (March 1945).
Iran Times, December 11-15,1972.
Kayhan International, June 20, 1975.
Keddie, N. "The Iranian Power Structure and Social Change 1800-1969." *International Journal of Middle East Studies,* January 1971.
Lambton, A. "Secret Societies and the Persian Revolution of 1905-1906." *St. Anthony's Paper* no. 4 (1958).
Lyman, Stanford M. and Marvin B. Scott. "Territoriality." *Social Problems* 12 (no. 4, 1967).
MacDonald, John S., and L. D. MacDonald. "Urbanization, Ethic Groups and Social Segregation." *Social Research* 29 (1972).
McLemore, Dale S. "Simmel's 'Stranger': A Critique of the Concept." *Pacific Sociological Review* (spring 1970).
Park, Robert E. "Human Migration and Marginal Man." *American Journal of Sociology* 33 (1928).
---. "Immigrant Community and Immigrant Press," *American Review* 3 (March-April 1925).
Perlmutter, A. "The Myth of the New Middle Class." *Comparative Studies in Sociology and History* 10 (196 7-68).
Riesman, David. "Some Observations Concerning Marginality." *Phylon* 12 (1951).
Ronaghi, Hosein Ali. "Moharerat-i-Pezeshgan" (physician migration), *Kayhan International* (June 16,1975).
Schutz, Alfred. "The Stranger." *American Journal of Sociology* 4 (1944).
---. "The Homecomer." *American Journal of Sociology* 10 (1945).
Siu, Paul C. P. "The Sojourner." *American Journal of Sociology* 56 (1952).
Stonequist, Everett. "The Problem of the Marginal Man." *American Journal of Sociology* 41 (July 1935).
Vidich, Arthur J. "Participant Observation and the Collection and Interpretation of Data." *American Journal of Sociology* 60 (July 1954-May 1955).
---, and Gilbert Shapiro. "A Comparison of Participant Observation and Survey Data," *American Sociological Review* 20 (February 1955)
Westoff, Leslie Aldridge. "Should We Pull Up the Gangplank? " *New York Times Magazine* (September 16,1973).

UNPUBLISHED MATERIAL

Bill, James. "The Iranian Intelligentsia: Class and Change." Ph.D. dissertation, Princeton University, 1968.
Borhanmanesh, Mohammad. "A Study of Iranian Students in Southern California," University of California at Los Angeles. Ed.D. dissertation, 1965.
Valipour, Iraj. "A Comparison of Returning and Non-Returning Iranian Students in the United States," Ed.D. dissertation, Columbia University, 1961.

PART III REFERENCES

Ansari, Moboud. 1977. "A Community in Process: The First Generation of the Iranian Professional Middle Class Immigrants in the United States." *International Review of Modern Sociology.* (pp. 8595)

Bozorgmehr, M. and G. Sabbagh. 1988. "High Status Immigrants: A Statistical Profile of Iranians in the United States." *Iranian Studies*. (pp. 5-13)

Haddad, 1987. *Islamic Values in the U.S.* New York: Oxford University Press, Inc. (p.51)

Immigration and Naturalization Service (1953-73) (1965 & 1986), *Iran Times*. July 14, August 21, September 21, October 32, 1987 November 18, 1988.

Muslim Journal. September 5, 1986

Reynolds, Fard, T. Ludwig. 1980 *The History of Religions*. Leuden J. Brill. (p. 147)

Riesman, David. 1951. "Some Observations Concerning Marginality." *Phylon* 12. (p. 3)

Stonequist, Everett. 1937. *The Marginal Man*. New York: Scribner. (p. 8)

Vidich, Arthur, and Michael W. Hughes. 1988. "Fraternization and Rationality in Global Perspective." *Politics, Culture and Society*. (p.246)

Weber, Max. 1968. *Economy and Society*. New York: Bedminister Press. (pp. 385-398)

INDEX